ONE WAY OUT

Where Pain Escorts Us Into the Presence of God

S. R. Nissi

One Way Out
Where Pain Escorts Us Into the Presence of God
by S. R. Nissi

Printed in the United States of America

ISBN 9780976966883

www.xulonpress.com

CONTENTS

ACKNOWLEDGEMENTS

This book is in honor of the one true living God. I stand in awe of you. I worship and surrender my life completely to you. It is because of Christ and His finished work on the cross, that I am able to live a life of freedom and abundance according to His perfect will for me. I give all glory to Him, who never left me nor failed me at any part of my life and healing journey. He is worth it all.

I want to extend a deep felt love, appreciation and gratitude toward my devoted prayer warrior and friend. I am grateful for your kindness and generosity that took me to the forefront of God's love and a new life. You sacrificed your time and energy, to invest in me through prayer, while teaching me excellent life skills and values. Your determination carried me through some of my darkest hours. Your vision of freedom for my life empowered me to hope in Christ again. Your example of love, compassion and grace escorted me into the arms of our Savior. Your gift of intercession was powerful and effective in my life. You are a beloved and faithful child of our Father. You are deeply loved by many, valued and respected by your circle of friends. You are a noble woman who stands in your own personal victory. Your friendship reflects the heart of Christ. Your gifts are used to set people free. You encourage others to be who they are called to be in Christ. You teach many to walk in the authority, power and knowledge of Him. I stand in agreement with you and declare "Love Wins". Thank you for your eternal investment in my life. You have impacted the lives of many for the Kingdom of God.

Thank you, my cherished friends who encircled me with joy, love and patience. I am very grateful for your grace as I endured through lengthy and difficult moments in my healing journey. Thank you for being men and women of God who reached out and generously supported me. You brought balance and perspective in my life when I needed it the most. Your friendships were vital during my healing process. I love each of you.

I recognize all the wonderful prayer warriors that stood with me to the end. Thank you for your incalculable hours of intercession over my life. This was a collective effort by all. I am grateful for the friendships that have developed over time, and will stand strong in the Lord for years to come. I value your friendships, talents, and gifts in Christ. Thank you for being men and women that seek the Lord, and walk in His truth and authority.

I am grateful for the newly developed relationships that God has so kindly intersected. I appreciate the support and kindness that has been extended through your love and developing friendships. I value the wisdom that has come from your personal testimonies of victory, and the joy you have brought to my heart.

Last but certainly not least, thank you to all those who guided me in this process of writing and giving me sound input and construction to make this complete. Thank you to my editor for generously devoting your time, thoughts and talents into making this a book of healing and a reason of hope for others. You are a cherished friend that has brought His life into all areas of mine. I love you deeply and appreciate your heart. This project is truly a team of joined forces, making this work complete.

INTRODUCTION

A friend once shared priceless wisdom with me. She said, "The pain that enters into our lives, as it inevitably will do, if taken to the Lord, it will be an experience that is priceless. It will be an experience that you will never desire to exchange. It is in those toughest hours that the pain will be an escort into the very presence of Christ". It is during those times walking so intimately in the presence of the Lord, that we begin to realize they are precious and undeniable, defining moments in our lives. It is in our suffering that we see the power of Jesus transform our lives. *But those who suffer he delivers in their suffering; he speaks to them in their affliction. (Job 36:15)*

This is a story that unfolds an excursion of my life. It depicts the accounts from early childhood through adulthood, unfolding horrifying events witnessed and experienced personally. It describes the invaluable lessons learned throughout my healing journey, while displaying the splendor of God's deep love for us. This is a story that demonstrates how a willing heart can become a powerful tool in overcoming such extensive abuse, violence, spiritual torment and a life destined for an unwelcome eternity. It describes a supernatural transformation from a life once lived in darkness, to a new life redeemed in His light. *I am the light of the world. Whoever follows me will never walk in darkness, but will have the light of life. (John 8:12)*

From early signs of abuse, to a troubled teen and growing into a bitter adult, this heartfelt true story explains: the power of forgiveness, repentance, releasing emotional and spiritual pain to God and journeys through portraits of freedom. It will inspire and encourage those who have been forced to face the trials of pain. It will give insight into God's love and plan he has for each of us to walk and live in freedom.

The prophetic visions will proclaim His truth and power, liberating those trapped in bondage. The detail of the visions will demonstrate His character of love, forgiveness, grace and healing for each of us.

This book will enlighten you to a life once forced and subjected to Satanic Ritual Abuse, living a same sex lifestyle and experiencing over a decade of aggressive and betraying relationships. From alcohol and violence, to anxiety, depression and suicide attempts, this entails the powers of darkness in which I wrestled, to the power of light I entered into. It will impart the truths that set me free of the demonic grip that held me in silence for many years. It led me down a path to God's almighty power, transformation, healing, freedom and a new testimony of encountering Christ.

Although only a few stories are mentioned throughout the 4-5 years of continued healing, this book describes some powerful encounters through visions of Christ bringing His words to our hearts. These visions were taken straight from the journals used in my healing sessions. They will lead you to a new understanding of just how much God desires to show us His love. It will take you from visions of hell to the expediential heights of heaven. This is the redeeming power He desires us to know, from the wonders of His throne room, to the sight of His eyes, and the heavenly angels, through a pathway of the "Highway to Holiness". It is a book inspired from the truth seeking journey that will impart His word, His miraculous works and His redeeming power.

CHAPTER 1

EVIDENCE OF A BROKEN FOUNDATION

I grew up in a simple, but nice family home in a small urban town in northern Illinois. For most families this would be a comfortable place to raise a "traditional" American family. The house was surrounded by other similar three bedroom ranch style homes with a typical one to two acre lot. This charming little neighborhood consisted of homes appealing to the eye. Each house was well kept with nicely trimmed and uniquely designed front yards. Most trees grew big and strong in stature. They provided shade from the blistering heat, while the various manicured landscape highlight the lush green yards. This eclectic neighborhood circled around a quarter mile of a roughly paved road, with multiple homes. Each family house was filled with an assortment of incomes, backgrounds and family members. It was a quiet neighborhood. Most families kept to themselves, with small amounts of interaction between the neighbors. However, on occasions there would be gathering over a summer BBQ and backyard games. Summers were grueling hot with humidity and bugs. Falls were filled with blissful colors of red, orange, golden yellows and fading green leaves. The crisp air began to warn of the harsh season ahead, but not before the pumpkins were brought home and the hot apple cider was gone, and the cupboards stocked with hot chocolate. Winters were relentless with the damp, moist air, followed by the freezing rains and often dangerous snowy ice storms. Most everyone endured the winter season indoors. The seasons were well marked by defining climate changes. Though the winters were often turbulant, the new emerging season of spring produced beautiful vibrant flowers and the scent of new life pushing through the ground. Hopeful buds blossomed leaves from flowering trees, while lush green hills embraced the sunshine of an approaching summer. For many, there were countless obvious reasons to endure the seasons in order to call quaint town, home.

For many, it was a wonderful and exciting place to raise a growing family. Several families foresaw the opportunity, full of potential growth, and booming with the local amenities. When I was young, I remember traversing through the undeveloped land to the local general store. I purchased a loaf of bread, some milk and an occasional treat, all for less than a couple of dollars. If we needed to run into the city, it was merely a fifteen minute drive. However, if we wanted to take a Sunday afternoon drive in the country, it was only five minutes the opposite direction. It was a surreal and pleasurable place. The town park was only a 5 minute walk which included swings, slides and a baseball field. What a treasure for a young person to explore during their juvenile years. It was small town America with all the space and fun any kid needed.

However, this little town people called home was far from what my heart called home. I moved to this house when I was seven to eight years old. My memories of this quaint town were assuredly different than most. Although this cute little upscale neighborhood was nestled in by appealing attractions such as: quality people, good schools and convenience, it was also surrounded by secluded groups of people who taught me a much different world.

The places few people visited were places that I was unfortunately forced to visit. Behind the facade of a "family neighborhood" stretched hidden pathways of destructive lies. At the side region of the homes ran a wooded area extending from our community touching into the quietness of the country. It was several miles of unsearched land. Railroad tracks divided parts of this wooded land. They extended beyond my investigation as a child. Near the railroad tracks lined a small single track trail paralleled below. If you followed this narrow path, it would lead you to this disturbing, little zone of land that very few traversed. It was vacant land by day. It was surrounded by a daunting quarry, with stone archways dueling as a bridge for the train that rarely passed by. Near the quarry, lied the town's trash dump, which very few people had any knowledge of its existence. Topping the town dump at the summit of the hill resided the town cemetery. The town cemetery seemed to house more people than the town itself. None the less, there were few visitors. The tall trees bordered around the cemetery. If you went in the opposite direction of the town dump, you would find a narrow and shallow stream that winding through a more dense section of the woods. This led into an open field of corn, tall grass and seclusion. As kids, most would be allured with the vast opportunities for the expansion of the imagination and to fill your days with limitless games. For me though, it was forbidden to participate in any adventures. I knew there was more to the enticing surroundings than most people would have ever expected. I didn't see these lands to be filled with life and escapades, rather a quarry that would represent far greater consequences, a dump filled with fear and a cemetery that nearly seized my own life at a young age.

In my family, a small town was known to have basic ideas about families and their involvements. In my family what was presented to the public eye, was far different than what occurred behind closed doors. In fact, my father prided himself in a well structured, tightly woven and happy family. He created this image for an outward appeal. We were a family who regularly attended church with smiles on our faces. We professed to be a strong Christian family. We attended Dad's meetings with perfect manners and a display of respect for the authoritarians. We were involved in the community, church and outreach organizations. Our record was squeaky clean with an image of perfection. Although, none of those qualities would be necessarily wrong; it was the heart and motive when the lights were dimmed, doors closed and nobody watching, that turned a family of amazement 'into a family of deep and hidden secrets.

We were so well defined by my father's control. It would be nearly impossible to prove that anything wrong could happen within our household. By the age of nine, I was experiencing life much different than your typical child. Life seemed far different than most kids my age. I dreamed of opportunities to be adopted by different people. Although I was surrounded by neighborhood kids, friends from sports and church, I felt completely alone and without a voice. I would withdraw and find solitude within my desire to draw. I would find an inner peace when I was around animals. Often it seemed at a young age I could tell there was a silent cry for help, yet there was an understanding that only in my dreams would someone come rescue me. Solutions as a nine year old child was not based on rational thinking, but engaged by any method to relieve the confusing deep ache that was growing in my heart. I somehow knew I was to remain silent over my pain and I didn't have any guidance of help. My inner and quiet plea for help was resolved by releasing my pain through self- mutilation. I would find ways when my heart was overwhelmed with inner turmoil to inflict damaging injuries to my body. Therefore if I physically hurt myself it would give me permission to release the inner emotional agony of my heart. I often expressed my cry through forcefully hitting my head against a wall or taking scissors and scraping my arm. Occasionally, I would take hammers and hit the side of my cheeks, just below my eyes. When I couldn't handle the pain anymore I would nearly collapse, tears overflowing, allowing the stream of sobs to be heard only by the void of my basement. This reclusive behavior continued and the risks became greater as I got older.

As a young child, I began to witness confusion between actions and words. I observed the pressure crumple the strength of my mom. She too, was beginning to show signs of the demented secrets held within a family. My father often raged in unpredictable tempers leaving my mother and myself alone in tears. His violent behavior was only demonstrated behind the walls of the family home. Publicly he was considered a wise and generous man. His words would occasionally speak of love, while his actions refuted my belief in his love. He was quick to raise his voice, closing his eyes and raising his hand with anger. He would rarely strike against us. But if I was caught with anything he considered against his beliefs, (smoking, drinking) it would only promise a severe punishment. It was a frightening control my father had over his family. He owned us. If we were disobedient it would assuredly guarantee a fearsome consequence. I squirmed when he hugged me. I resisted internally when there was physical contact. I worried anxiously when I had to be alone with him. I hated the phrase, "daddy's little girl".

When I was in middle school, opportunities expanded for my parents to take on more children in their "perceived" happy, little home. My parents decided to open their doors to foster children. After all, it would provide great opportunities to continue to polish their great reputation. Perhaps it was good intentions on their part, but what pioneered as good intentions, rapidly declined to an alarming outcome.

I am not sure the exact age of our first two children, a boy and a girl, both younger than myself. I remember the social worker arrived with these two broken kids, and a couple of grocery sacks filled with their belongings. It was over a period of time that they lived with us, when saddening events began to fill their hearts as the true, but hidden identity of my family began to emerge.

It was an evening around our maple kitchen table, that dinner was served. I remember my mom, myself and the little foster boy, Ricky sitting at the table. Perhaps, others were dismissed, or gone for the evening. I had finished dinner and was bringing my plate to the sink to wash it. The kitchen sink and the table were not far apart. I washed my dish, rinsed it and then dried it with the towel. It didn't take me to long to finish my work in order to be dismissed. As I left the kitchen area, I realized Ricky was still sitting at the table and had a few more items, mostly vegetables on his plate. He didn't seem interested in eating and even voiced to my mom, he didn't like vegetables.

I left the kitchen and returned a short time later, to check in on Ricky and cross through the kitchen area. Our kitchen was central to the basement, backyard sliding glass doors and the living room. As I walked near the kitchen, I could tell my mom's demeanor was beginning to change. Ricky was still seated, this time I noticed his chair was much closer to the table pinning him in his seat. I stood there for only a brief moment before my mom seemed to escalate in frustration. She demanded Ricky to finish his meal before he could get up. I saw his lower lip quiver and tears well up in his eyes. I started to observe the battle of wills take place. He refused to eat his dinner, and she was determined for him to finish the few remaining vegetables on his plate. I stood off in a distance away from the main spectacle. My mom stomped her feet to the table. Pointing her finger she was insistent on him eating his food. This time she was taking action to her words. She pinched his nose as he was beginning to squirm, and she literally yelled at him until he opened his mouth. At this time, his mouth was tightly shut, until he recognized he could no longer breathe. When he took a gasp for air, my mom was quick to shovel the food down his throat and then forcefully close his mouth until he swallowed. When he swallowed the food, she removed her hand from his nose allowing him to breathe. She gave him another chance to finish the food on his own. She sat watching his every move. When he didn't make any obvious signs to eat on his own will, it became clear her intentions were to force feed him again. This time he was crying. She tightly pinched his nose and forced the food down his throat. However, with the mixture of emotions, and an obvious dislike to the food, he quickly regurgitated the food back onto the table.

By this time, my stomach was upset. I was easily unnerved, with anger rising and confusion setting into my heart and mind. I took a few steps back. I wanted to stop the madness, but with fear exhibited on my face, one look from my mom pierced my soul. Without any words communicated from my mom, I knew her look meant don't you dare do anything. In fact, I knew it would have been better for me to leave the room, but I could not. I was frozen, and unable to move as several emotions welled up within me.

It was a moment that turned from frustration into violence. I watched helplessly as Ricky was forced to taste a spoonful of evil. The food that was forced to go down, went down, but within a moment violently came back up. This time it was the entire dinner. My mom was appauled and in a moment of fury grabbed the back of his head and forced his face down into the pile of throw up. Ricky flailed his arms and feet and fought the pressure of my mom's hand over the back of his head. He came up for a breath with a face covered in his own vomit. She demanded that he now eat his own pile of vomit.

By now, I was beyond sick, not only with the mess, but with the disgust of my mom's behavior. I stood in the background and watched silently, fearful of my mom's behavior and saddened at Ricky's turmoil.

He continued to fight and resist. My mom scooped up the mess on the table and continued to forcefully and vengefully demand he eat his vomit. Ricky resigned to the demands of my mom and reluctantly opened his mouth and the sour taste of his own vomit was forced down his throat. Although the entire pile of throw up was not consumed, I watched the wickedness of my mom break the heart and will of a young boy. All this happened in order to maliciously make a point for him to eat his food, and submit to her power. After several horrid bites of his vomit, the unfortunate and spiteful ordeal was over.

Although Ricky was forced to endure this wretched food crisis, it was ill-fated that he would experience an even greater wicked episode within our home. It was an evening when my father was gone late into the night. The remainder of the family was gathered in the living room. The youngest little foster girl had gone to bed. My brother, mom, myself and Ricky were still awake. We were sitting in our small living room. We had a plaid orange and brown couch along the main side of the wall, a brown recliner seat, and a black painted rocking chair, that sat on each side of our stone walled fireplace. It was a night I will never forget. Ricky had somehow in a small and minor way disobeyed. It was to be expected of any foster child coming from a broken and distraught family. It is known that there will be some issues that arise and corrections that will need to be made. However, this was no ordinary disciplinarian action… this was cruel punishment. In an irrational and illogical manner my mother took it upon herself to overpower Ricky and his own will. In the chill of an early evening, we had established a well burning fire inside the cove of our fireplace. The flames were intense and the pop of the wood crackling became louder. My mother grabbed Ricky by his arms and forced him to sit on the stone hearth in front of the fire. The only thing that remained between him and the fire was a thin, metal, woven screen that slid in front of the fire itself. He was forced to sit less than a foot away from the burning, hot fire. He sat there with his right side and a portion of his back to the fireplace. He was already crying from the fear that raced through his tiny and fragile body. My mom sat in the corner enforcing her rules with a very low and controlled voice.

I will not forget the emotions that roused inside me. In fact, as I mention this story, it seems like yesterday that I witnessed the mind control and power of evil people. My heart was pounding and an anger boiling. I didn't know what to do. I knew if I stopped this torment, I too, could be the next victim. I was young and did not want to combat against my mom. I knew I had to remain silent. Somehow, this fear paralyzed me. I witnessed a horrific event unfold before my eyes.

His crying escalated into convulsive sobs. His sobs were beginning to turn to screams. My mom got up from her chair, and declared the idea that if he stopped screaming he could get up and go to bed. Nearly impossible to dismiss his pain, he continued to cry. This led her to blame him, claiming he brought this punishment upon himself.

The pain was becoming unbearable. On occasion, he would scoot his little body away from the fire to the edge of the hearth. It would be in those little moments, he would try to find relief. My mom stood in front of him pushing him back, demanding obedience and silence from him. How could he stop crying or be silent? His legs were slowly receiving severe burns from sitting so closely to the fire. Did she not know? His little chest expanding and releasing rapidly as he tried to stop his own torment and punishment that was exceedingly worse than anything he deserved.

Finally, the pain of sitting in front of the fireplace had ended. It was within moments that my mom forced him into a cold shower, trying to hide the obvious mistake she made. It was as if another personality snapped her out a cruel perpetrator, into a person that realized the extent of damage that was done. The exposure of his evident burns would give him the freedom he needed; a ticket out of our house.

It was shortly after the suffering that it was evident he needed medical attention. It was a phone call and medical attention that brought awareness to the social worker. She promptly removed these two children from our home. He was released with the lie that Ricky burned himself while taking a scolding hot shower. Regardless of the lie, or the lies that he was forced to tell, his freedom from our house, was now a welcomed reality. Although, I was happy for both of the young kids, I won't forget the sadness and jealousy their departure meant for me. I remained in an evil and unstable house.

The "accident" was never investigated and therefore released. I entered a season that allowed several kids come and go in our house. We had foreign exchange students arrive and depart. Even young men and women seeking refuge during ministry internships stayed in our home. Regardless, all students and newly arriving children were greeted with warm smiles and a persona of a happy and generous family. Yet, several kids left with an uneasy experience. Some experiences were voiced, while others left in silence.

Junior High

By the time I was in junior high, I experienced verbal abuse, witnessed physical abuse, and felt sexually violated. However, though it was unspoken I knew there was a deeper pain in my heart, and it was birthing dangerous emotions. I was extremely conflicted and confused. I could feel darkness of vengeful anger fill me. I contemplated the value of an empty life, in comparison to a false sense of pleasure by way of death. I was taking on some power greater than myself. Perhaps it came from the abuse or the example I continued to experience from my parents. My father's unpredictable behavior would cause dangerous arguments between him and members of the family. He was impulsive and violent with his words and sometimes his actions. I hated being alone with him. I often tried to avoid his presence. He would snap into a different person instantly, and without warning. His uninvited intrusions into the bathroom, while I was showering alarmed me. His power to overrule any boundary I set would diminish my words. He paraded around the house with little clothes on and often made my skin shiver when he hugged me or told me he loved me. I never trusted him, and was repulsed by any gestures of touch or love. I never felt safe at home and frequently didn't sleep at nights in fear of his unwelcomed arrivals in my bedroom. I was told to be quiet. It was common for my dad to be quick with his tongue. He would flare reckless words such as; he is ashamed of me, and didn't want to call me his own daughter. He hurled insults such as; I was a slut, fat, ugly, psycho, worthless and the worst one of all; I wouldn't amount to anything. He fought me to the ground, wrenching my arm backwards. He would corner me against the wall with a finger pointing at me. He would scream at me. My parents would threaten to kill my life. He would kick me out of the house consistently, and then demand I return to the house before anyone found out. His reputation was always hanging in the balance. He tried hard maintaining a stature of prestige. He couldn't afford the mistake of his family crumbling, as he sought the high road of his agendas. He walked a fine line of power and control mingled with insanity and devestation.

There were countless times my family and I walked on eggshells in trepidation of the uncertain moods my dad displayed. Other times, his character demonstrated an outgoing, intelligent business man who was involved in his family activities. That mixed behavior left me bewildered in confusion. My boundaries, personality and identity were shattered at the whim of a violent, confusing man. He had more than a hot temper. He had an evil presence that repelled me and my friends.

Despite the sudden bursts of his unpredictable behavior, my family still held to the legalistic spiritual and moral convictions. It was unheard of to miss a Sunday lesson at our small church. We could not miss attending Sunday school in the morning, followed by a 1-2 hour service and then needing to attend an evening service. In addition to our Sunday regiment, it was certain we would be seen later in the week at least once, if not twice for the choir, elder and youth activities. There is nothing wrong with the desire to attend church and various activities. What concerned me was the ambiguity that was beginning to rise in my heart, between my parent's motives and God's heart. How could parents go to church and act perfectly fine, yet have so many people fooled by a false character? How could I trust God, Christians and my parents? Although that was quite difficult to understand, the real monster would arise later, exposing the spirit behind the legalistic mindset of this perfect, church going family.

High School

By the time I entered high school; I was confused, hated life and felt an overwhelming sense of emptiness. In fact by the early age of 13 or 14, I already seriously contemplated suicide. Although I felt empty, I was fortunate to be surrounded by friends and teachers who cared for me. It was apparent my circle of friends and my involvement in sports kept me alive. By now, I had a distorted view of life, God, love, relationships and myself. At the age of 15, I would engage in anything that promised to void out my anger and sorrows. I began drinking at any opportunity that presented itself, and smoked whenever I was able to hide it. At the age of 16, I tampered with dangerous drugs, and only continued down a destructive road full of reckless choices. By the age of 17, I struggled to gain some kind of control in my life. I found my power by controlling my food consumption. I battled with three devestating eating disorders. I struggled to hold any positive attitudes towards life. Because sports suppressed most of the pain, I was able to function in life. The young age of 17 brought about a combat of risky choices. My weight reduced down to a hazardous number. I rarely slept from nightmares and fears. I would frequently awake with an unknown restless night. My parents threatened to place me in a psychiatric home. They controlled every decision and seldom allowed any freedoms in my life.

At the age of 18, I found myself in a dwindling pool of pain. I was alone and knew where my dad's old revolver gun was hidden. It was a point of no return. I was ready to end this early life filled with undeniable emotional pain. I slipped one bullet in the revolving chamber and spun it around. The chamber stopped. I placed my finger on the trigger. I took a deep breath and felt the spiritual and emotional anguish in my heart. I simply did not want to deal with life anymore. There was no escape to this pain. My body pressed into the couch in the basement and quietness filled the air. No one was there to stop me. My heart pounded. I was determined to end this misery. Was the bullet in the slot that would end my life? Without further delay, I raised the gun to the right side of my forehead. All that flashed before me was an empty life filled with anger, hatred, injustice, pain, tears, and unanswered questions. I was alone in my grievance, without help or anyone to lead me in a different direction. My finger pulled, and the tension of the trigger was released. A soft click silenced my thoughts for a brief moment, when I realized my life didn't end. I was confused, slightly happy yet still filled with pain. I spun the chamber again. I was determined to not live an agonizing life. The chamber had stopped spinning, and I was once again dancing with destiny. I lifted the gun to my head, and in that moment the phone rang. I took a deep breath and remained holding the gun as I answered the phone. It was a friend of mine. She was calling to invite me to a party. We chatted for a brief moment, when her voice seemed to soften. She asked if I was doing okay. I assured her I was fine, and continued our course of conversation. As I was speaking to her I sat back down on the couch fiddling with the loaded gun. I lifted my right hand, and with my finger on the trigger spun the revolver around like a western cowboy on TV. A loud explosion nearly burst my ears. My friend shouted with fear asking, "Are you okay"? Placing the gun on the floor, I calmed her down and convinced her that I was okay. After having a long conversation with her, I too realized I was not yet ready for my life to end. Somehow, I need to manage this pain and seek help.

CHAPTER 2

YOUNG INDEPENDENCE

Nearing the end of high school, I reflected on my years. I had found a few exciting and cherished moments with friends along with wonderful athletic opportunities. I was now greatly anticipating my next move. It would be a move out of the house and away from the darkness. Somehow through high school I was able to maintain a decent attendance record and grade point average. However, my GPA fell short of the standard requirements for Division I college scholarships. It didn't bother me, because I didn't really care about college. I cared about leaving my home. I felt that if going to any college would get me out of the house; it would be good enough for me. It was not what my parents wanted, but for now, they had no other choice. I started going to a junior college an hour away, and continued my life. I abandoned my family and God, to enjoy a life of partying and careless behaviors.

My parents had labeled me the crazy, black sheep of the family. They found it astonishing that they could raise a child with such poor behavior. I always knew the fruit did not fall far from the tree. Because I was now old enough to start making some choices, it became evident their style of raising children, was deranged. Although my father had a strong influence over my life, I was now out of arms reach. However, because his influence remained, he insisted that I seek help through an unbiased church counselor. He thought, surely his church rules would save me. I was to blame for my erratic behavior. After all,

I thought I would only live out what was modeled to me. Yet when I was thrown into an adult world with only wounds in my heart and no quality guidance, it was not a surprise that the quality of decisions in my life also lacked wisdom. Therefore, since signs of problems in my life were arising, it was apparent I needed to seek support from a counselor. Once again, under the demand of my father, I was forced into counseling, while attending my first year of college. However, the counseling sessions took on an unexpected twist. It was a mystery unfolding. I agreed to honestly speak of my pain. I also concurred with her solutions for helping me. Over several consultations, her concerns grew more alarming. She rapidly made the effort to include my parents within the session. It was after my consent, of course. I felt, why not? They forced me to do this, so sure, include them as well. A professional counselor with minimal amount of information looked at my record, searched my heart, received honest answers and quickly felt the need to address my parents. Finally, my "craziness", according to my parents, was professionally clarified and validated to be a reason for further concern and guidance. With the truth being exposed, my dad immediately terminated my counseling. My parents presence, angry looks and stern postured told me to remain silent. It was not to be mentioned again. It was a posture I knew well by now. It was a non-verbal threat of an undesirable penalty. I was discouraged in my heart. I thought I would have an opportunity to be understood. Perhaps, someone could validate my pain. My mind swirled with confusion. I thought my parents wanted me to overcome the empty void in my heart. Why would they remove something good in my life? I didn't understand, yet shrugged my shoulders and moved on.. Their plan to prove their point that I was crazy, and possibly needed hospitalization back-fired, showing the real concern was them.

Living far enough away from home, I made the decision I would no longer attend church. This was my first freedom exercised. I was disgusted at "church people" and God. I only saw "Christians" to be hypocritical, judgmental and abusive. People I could not trust. I was belittled by them, ridiculed and controlled by the legalistic laws. It seemed that the decisions I made from the abuse, were all the wrong decisions according to the "church". Most of them were fake. I was on my own now. I was going to live a life that felt right to my heart.

It was shortly after a life of "freedom" that I slipped into a harsh life abandoned from God. I knew who God was. He was the creator over all. To me, He was a huge "dad" figure that represented punishment, law, cruelty, confusion, condemnation and judgment. I knew I could never do enough to please Him or my earthly dad. After all, my earthly father constantly said, "You are going to hell". My dad would say, "You deserve hell". So, to me, what difference would it make? If I am already doomed for hell, why not live a life of fleshly pleasures? I viewed God wanting to burn my soul. Although I went to church, it was out of obligation. It wasn't because I felt a connection with Christ. I knew His laws, not His love. Why now would I understand His love? I wanted to find love. I wanted to find acceptance. I wanted to find laughter and fun. I could not endure the weight of more pain. God, Christianity and my parents represented pain, betrayal, belittlement, inadequacy, confusion, resentment and judgment. It was time for me to have some fun.

It was not long after I assumed this role of freedom that I found myself in peculiar places. I searched for love but quickly found myself in a lifestyle that would captivate 11 years of my life. I grew to distrust men. I resented a weak woman mentality. Therefore, what became appealing to me was a strong, figure that cared for my heart. A person that would listen, understand and validate the agony inside. I wanted to connect with someone and share life's simple and deep moments. However, what attracted me was the same sex gender. Of course I knew the church disowned these people, but I was never going to tell. It was another secret held deep within my heart. It was a chance for love. It was a chance to trust again. It was my way of allowing my heart to come alive. I found a relationship that didn't judge and didn't accuse me. I found a relationship that believed me, empowered me and allowed some laughter to enter in to my life.

I began to realize the relationship lacked boundaries. It was what I knew. After all, my father never respected any of my boundaries. His intrusions into my bedroom left me sickened, and violated. My mother had to know, but her weak disposition never stood against my father's temper. I guess it was only to be expected for her to remain silent. Therefore, when I became enmeshed, searching for identity through this relationship, it was no wonder I became co-dependent. Boundaries were constantly broken. My fragile identity was camouflaging with her personality. The love changed into a false security and my world began to crumble with the relationship. Violence emerged, betrayal and abandonment settled into my heart.

Once again, I submitted to the overwhelming pain. I attempted to take my life into my own hands and placed my fate at the doorsteps of death. I mixed chemical poisons with over the counter pills. This time, it was an unrelenting pain of a supernatural power pumping my stomach in order to keep me alive. I did not know what happened. I only vaguely remember lying lifeless on a cold bathroom floor for a couple of days. It was a breath of life that kept me seeing the light of the next day.

My parents found out, and quickly remedied the relationship. They moved me home. I thought it was a gesture of kindness. However, it turned into a heartache filled with rejection, shame and guilt. The shame of my parent's embarrassment was forced upon me. Their move was only to protect themselves from the exposure of my behavior. The routine of abuse continued. The debilitating words surrendered me under their control. The unwanted visits from my dad through the night, started again. They enforced silence upon my heart and the entire situation was to be forgotten. They voiced a very harsh and critical opinion of me. They did not want to help, or understand. They wanted it to go away. I must forget my pain and pretend to be a loving daughter.

I was determined to escape from my parents and sought to finish college far from home. I received a basketball scholarship at a Christian college. I thought surely this would get them off my back. I had forcefully rejoined and attended church with a smile on my face. However, signing a letter of intent for basketball, and study at a Christian college, would appease their demands, and give me some hope again.

I moved far from home, out of their sight and control. I skipped the chapel requirements and found myself at college parties. I didn't seem to matter, as long as you didn't get caught. I sought adventure and fun. Near my senior year in college I found myself tied into another hopeless relationship. I hid it from the eyes of my teammates, coach and professors. However the pain in my eyes caused concern among my closer friends. I thought this relationship would be different entering into it. I was more mature and stronger in character. I was not going to shy away from conflict. However, this relationship quickly turned into turmoil. I was cheated on, lied to and betrayed. Out of complete desperation, I begged for this relationship not to end. The result was nothing short of expected pain, continual betrayal, and violent physical and verbal abuse. I was at rock bottom. I struggled to attend class and my teammates noticed the extreme pain I was trying to overcome. I frantically found a gun with a loaded clip. I ran out the door, driving away in my rusted old car. I parked in a vacant lot, next to some softball fields. Surveying the manicured fields, I reflected on my empty life. Although I strongly desired to pull the trigger, I could not find the strength to do it. I sat, weeping over my life.

Even though I felt I was hiding my pain, an observant friend advised me to seek a counselor's help. I rolled my eyes and sighed. I thought to myself I have been there, done that. I kindly replied, "No thanks". She persisted with her idea. She was going to a counselor and felt I would greatly benefit from this lady's wisdom and guidance.

Transition Into Salvation

By now, I was ending my last year in college. My friend removed me from the unstable living condition and desired to help me through a journey of healing. I resided with her and another teammate while transitioning into a new phase of my life. I softened to the idea of counseling, and within days, the counselor herself called me. I arranged a time to meet with her. This was my third or fourth counselor by now. I was reluctant and mischievous. I wanted to test her and the waters before I would ever consider sharing my heart. It took a great extent of time. We talked about daily life, relational problems and other easy topics. We finally got to the subject of rape. I trusted her enough to expel the details of my rape. I was seventeen and was ignorant to the casual idea of a walk. Well, the walk with the college football player turned into a illicit incident of forced sex. I would watch her response. I would evaluate her body language. I would determine the amount of information I would divulge. I wanted to be in control. She thought to try group therapy, only to escalate my anxiety. Therefore, she resumed to individual therapy. She was the first to provide a strong, deep, honest and pure love. I found her intriguing. I liked her. I knew this relationship was profoundly impacting my life. Her extensive wealth of knowledge combated my resistant behavior. She demonstrated a tough love. I knew she was a believer, yet she never pushed God on me. I was fine with that. I signed paperwork that I was a Christian. I believed in God. I didn't say what I thought of Him, just that I believed in God. After all, lots of people believe in God, but like me, do they really know Him? Several years went by. My counselor was often my only friend. She kept me alive.

I had transitioned from the college life into reality. It was a rocky road, leading pathetic attempts in relationships. I failed more than a few times. I still seemed to cycle through unstable moods. I questioned God, who He was and why I felt so alone. I was still in counseling and found myself in uncharted waters. A good friend introduced me to some other really neat people. I found myself laughing. I found myself in the company of love and kindness. I wasn't being judged, though I still had my moments of rebellion. Instead, I was encircled by developing friendships that deeply cared for me. And to my surprise they were Christians. I was amazed. They knew my history of darkness. They knew I would go out and drink. They even knew the preference of my relationships. I was baffled.

The relationships developed and life seemed manageable. My friends attended church on a regular basis. They invited me every Sunday. I refused every Sunday. It was a spontaneous moment that an invitation was extended to attend a church concert. It was local artists and free food was included. I am a woman that will not turn down free food. Therefore, I thought the good outweighed the bad. I decide to go.

The concert was small. It was a quiet and intimate environment. The music was soothing and really invited my spirit to join in. A man stood up in a quiet moment of worship. The instruments softly lulled in the background. The lights were dimmed and a peace covered the congregation. He began to speak a convicting, but loving word from the Lord. I quietly listened to what he was saying and in no time I felt like it was directly aimed for my ears to hear. My heart was pounding. I began to feel my mind fade and my spirit rise. Tears welled in my eyes, and He spoke with power and authority. Was anyone else listening, or was this just for me? How did he know exactly what I needed to hear? He paused, and then sat down. The room was silent with the exception of a few soft sniffles. I saw this moment to be an opportunity of a quick escape from conviction. Maybe I could hide the fact that his words just pierced right to my heart. I found myself dashing for a secluded place in the bathroom. I opened the bathroom door in hopes to take a deep breath, and pretend that never happened. However, my friend was quietly trailing behind me. I was unable to hide; instead I had to face the reality of a disordered life.

The concert experience was one of the first knocks I heard on the front door of my heart. However, it certainly would not be the last. These wonderful Christian friendships developed overtime. I began to desire a little more understanding of God's love towards me. I slowly initiated asking questions and evaluating my heart. My personal counseling was going well. I realized I was surrounded by many people who deeply cared and loved me. I was embarking upon exciting adventures in uncharted waters. This season of my life was evolving to good things and opportunities. I realized surrounding myself in a strong community was a vital role in my healing and growing process.

Life as I knew it was beginning to fade away. An afflicted past seemed to slowly dissipate. The sickness, anxiety, depression and suicidal thoughts were not as customary. Joy and laughter seemed more consistent. Life was transforming a little at a time. I felt stronger and more confident.

Now at 30 years old, life was going better. I was more stable than any other time of my life. I had not accepted Christ as my personal Savior, but was carefully watching my community of friends, closely. I observed their interactions and love towards each other. I witnessed the faith that filled them, despite circumstantial events. I examined their choices. I experienced an unconditional love through their friendships. I was cautiously opening my heart. However, it is an event none of us will forget, that compelled my heart to change forever. It was the shattering news of world events that brought about a life changing decision for me. Shortly after our nation witnessed the devastating terrorist attacks on September 11, 2001, I made a life altering decision. I had scriptural knowledge in my head. I knew on my own merit I didn't deserve Heaven. No- one does enough good deeds to make it in to

Heaven. How would you ever know what would be enough to enter into Heaven? I knew there was a Sovereign Creator. My heart and mind were conflicted. My mind knew what was right, but my heart was too darkened by the past, to see light. I knew there were countless events in my life when I blamed God. But, was He the one to blame? I hated Him, but did I really know Him? Now, I have witnessed love. It was good. I experienced grace, peace, and joy. My friends were different. He was beginning to show me He was a different God, than what I knew as a child. I searched my heart and found myself in a place of emptiness. Watching the catastrophic events unfold minute by minute was overwhelming me. What was next? I knew if I were to die the next day, I would be uncertain of my destiny. I decided that was an eternal question demanding an answer. I was playing with fire, if I didn't know my eternal destination. Without hesitation, I abandoned my thoughts of doubt and went with the need of my heart. I invited Christ into my life. I surrendered to Him and asked Him to be the Lord of my life. His word states; *for God so loved the world that he gave his one and only Son, that whoever believes in him shall not perish but have eternal life. Vs. 21: But whoever lives by the truth comes into the light, so that it may be seen plainly that what he has done has been done through God. (John 3:16)* Literally the same day His light entered into my heart a heavy spirit left my soul. I knew it was only the beginning of an unknown journey. I knew I would never regret this decision.

This powerful moment in time brought about a destination change, and a peace within my heart. I repented for my sin. Therefore, I needed to allow God to move me in a different route. Although it was a powerful transformation from within, outwardly I was going to encounter enormous changes. My relational involvements gradually divided. There were many nights filled with tears and many days of heart ache. Although, there were many attempts before to remove myself from the patterns of my past, this time, I was determined, with the help of God, to persevere. I studied the word of God. I verbalized my pain to those helping me. I chose not to participate in the former events that would tempt me. It was trying, but through the support of friendships, and the power of the Holy Spirit, I was able to gradually forget what was behind and press forward to claiming glorious freedom. *Brothers, I do not consider myself yet to have taken hold of it. But one thing I do: Forgetting what is behind and straining toward what is ahead. (Philippians 3:13)*

Over time, I meditated on the Bible. It wasn't studying the Bible to memorize it, rather to know His word in my heart. The comfort of His Holy Spirit empowered me to change from broken relationships to a Holy relationship. It was only by receiving the power of the Holy Spirit filled with love that I was able to transfer from a worldly love to a passionate spiritual life giving love. He knew the details of my heart and life, and loved me. By accepting His love, and simply living in His love, I was satisfying the very core and nature of His character. God is love. This is His plan for us, to live in His love. It wasn't transitioning to another partner. It was not trying to do something or find something; it was realizing I was found as a new creation in His love.

CHAPTER 3

TRANSFORMING OLD TO NEW

My Christian walk had its trials. I did not know what to expect. I guess I knew it would not be easy. But this time, I knew that His power was within me. Therefore, I knew I was never alone. During the first three years of a young and growing Christian, I witnesses God's miraculous work of provision and healing. It was amazing. My faith grew stronger. During some desperate moments, God proved His faithfulness. I witnessed immediate answers in prayer. My relationship with Christ grew deeper in love and trust. Eventually, there was very little trace of my past. Instead I was growing in new opportunities of hope, and a future with Christ. *For I know the plans I have for you," declares the Lord, "plans to prosper you and not to harm you, plans to give you hope and a future. Then you will call upon me and come and pray to me, and I will listen to you. You will seek me and find me when you seek me with all your heart. I will be found by you," declares the Lord. (Jeremiah 29:11-14)*

Although, new friendships and opportunities were springing forth, there was still a lot of work that was being exposed in my heart. I found myself denying some emerging pain. I would set the pain and confusion aside and immersed myself in His word. However, His word seemed to bring conviction in my heart. He was showing me I needed to press further into areas of my past. He drew me closer to His heart. He wanted to guide me in His written word, and intimately seek His heart; the author of truth. He was pursuing me in a passion of love, and His next step was about to be revealed.

I found myself sitting in the basement of my friend's house, where I was currently renting a room. I was in a routine of prayer and quiet time before the Lord. I read some passages from the Bible. In an instant, I knew the Lord was beginning to expose some hidden walls in my heart. I opened the Bible directly to Isaiah 54. *Though the mountains be shaken and the hills be removed, yet my unfailing love for you will not be shaken nor my covenant of peace be removed, says the Lord, who has compassion on you. Vs 11 O afflicted city lashed out by storms and not comforted, I will build you with stones of turquoise, your foundations with sapphires. I will make your battlements of rubies, your gates of sparkling jewels, and all your walls of precious stones. (Isaiah 54: 10-13)* I was stunned with the exact words of this scripture. I did not recall reading this passage before now. My head seemed to know the Lord was speaking to me. His truth was piercing the darkness of my past. His words seemed to evoke a rumbling in my heart that had not yet been heard. His eternal salvation was deposited in my heart, but plans of restoration were now taking shape in my life. His gracious love shook the foundations of my heart. His word was telling me; His love will not be shaken for me. A troubled heart that was not comforted will be restored. He will make my foundations solid. I will be comforted and established in His righteousness. My heart was conflicted. His word brought peace and comfort, but my internal mode raged with anger. My heart strongly desired to resist. Fear and anger overcame me. What does all this mean? I didn't quite understand my response. On one hand, His word brought peace; on the other hand, something within me powerfully opposed the idea of healing. This internal battle was overwhelming. I collapsed on the couch. Tears streamed down my face, as a familiar pain stabbed my heart. It was that deep heartache and grief I had tried to avoid for years. It was the unspoken nightmares and flashbacks of unanswered questions, which I kept suppressing. He wanted to do a deep work; one which I knew would require hard work.

I sat bewildered on the couch, hemmed in by an empty, quiet and lonely basement. I recognized the crossroad before me. My choices were very distinguished in my mind. One choice would require me to compromise myself, and an intimacy with the Lord. I could continue my life of denial and compromise all the Lord would have for me. I could continue down this path of frustration. I could allow my past to interfere with my relationship with the Lord. Or I could choose a path that would demand a sacrifice on my part. It would assuredly be a work of the Lord on His timing, not my own. It would insist my time and energy. It would carve a new path, promising a rocky road ahead. I sat sunken into the couch, and lowered my head into my trembling hands. I took a deep breath in, then exhaling the heaviness of my decision. I wrestled with the reality of walking in the unknown. How could I continue? Did I already have enough evidence of a disturbing past? The healing I experienced brought life to me. How could I deny myself and Christ the opportunity for more? Yet, the acknowledgment of turmoil in my heart was an obvious sign; this would not be an easy task. Can I handle the pain? Am I ready for this? What does this entail? The first choice would leave me incomplete. The second choice felt like I was compromising my plans and dreams. The main question to ask myself was; who is more important in my life? Jesus or me. If I had all my dreams, would it be worth it without God in my life. The obvious answer was no. If I lived a luke warm life with Christ, would I be happy? Again, the answer was no. I am a black and white person. I realized I am more passionate about what Christ wants for me, then what I want for me. I chose to be obedient to the season God planned before me.

I surrendered and agreed to set my plans aside and humbly accept what He desires to show me. I stopped reading the Bible for a moment; while broken memories of my past filled my mind. I knew that I could not suppress the hidden insecurities, pain and lack of identity anymore. I knew by now, the nightmares, flashbacks had more to tell than I allowed and that it was obvious I still needed help. It was time to quit trying to be what others wanted me to be and resolve to who God wanted me to be. It was time to set aside all the intentions I had of who I wanted to be and humbly allow God to mold me into the very creation of who He made me to be. I sighed and agreed to once again admit myself into counseling.

I was both reluctant and excited to start this journey. Without any knowledge of the extensive time it would entail, I knew it was all or nothing. I needed to put my whole effort into this part of my life, in order for me to live a life beyond merely existing in a Christian box. I wanted a quality and passionate life. I wanted to abandon myself for an intimate knowledge of Christ's love and heart. I buckled down and realized this would require determination and tenacity.

CHAPTER 4

DISCERNING VOICES

As I journeyed through healing, it seemed essential to know and understand God's love and heart for me. Though I knew there were countless ways God could speak, I also was very open to making sure I knew God's voice. I wanted to be positive through the difficult times. With every human capability, I wanted to follow His leading. I began to really meditate on His infallible truth. I sought Him, fasted and fervently prayed. I spent moments before going to bed praying. I spent hours awake in quiet time seeking Him. I spent days at work asking the Lord, "What is truth?" I want to hear your voice. I want to know truth. I want to experience your love. The word of God became my bread. As I read the word quietly, and in Bible studies, I began to come across specific studies on hearing His voice. I sought counsel on how to hear God's voice. I began to understand that God truly desires to speak to our hearts through his voice. By quieting my mind, and being still and in touch with His heart, I began to know His voice. It was out of relationship that I could hear Him speak to my heart. I began to realize that I needed to cultivate an atmosphere to hear His voice. Sometimes it was protecting my space and time in a quiet secluded place in order for me to silence the outside distractions and have quality time with the Lord. Other times it was fostering stillness in my heart and in my mind in order to hear from Him. I knew that spending time in His presence would sharpen the ears and eyes of my heart to be attentive to his voice. It was when I slowly lost my times alone with him that my discernment became dull. It was important for me to walk in humility, and continually ask God to cleanse me of anything that would hinder me from hearing His voice. I wanted a life of purity, seeking Him and His truth at every cost. It was the air I needed to breathe. I would often wait patiently in His presence, refusing all obvious lies from the enemy, and any perceptions from myself or others about my journey of seeking truth. Just as He says in his word, those who seek Him will find him. He found me. *Ask and it will be given to you; seek and you will find; knock and the door will be opened to you. For everyone who asks receives; he who seeks finds; and to him who knocks, the door will be opened. (Matthew 7:7-8)*

Over time, I was able to separate the voice of Satan and the voice of God. The more you know Jesus, the easier it is to discern between the different voices. I know the voice of God is one of love, teaching and conviction. I know His voice, because I know the heart of the One who speaks. When you know Christ's heart, you are better able to know what would come out of His mouth and His heart for you. His heart is not one of condemnation. God's voice is one that will always bring you to a deeper relationship with Him. It may not always be what you want to hear. Regardless, His voice will be a soft whisper that will return your eyes, heart and direction back to Him. It will be one that will speak softly to you in a way that other voices or people cannot affect you. It seems to go deep within to the secretive places of your heart, when no one else is looking. His voice without doubt will always bring truth. He cannot lie. His voice will bring a peace, even when the situation or decision seems to not be at peace. His voice will dismantle lies. His voice comes in a softness and gentleness even if there are corrections that need to be made. His voice will always align with His written word. His heart and His voice is always for you in a way of perfect love.

Satan's voice is often a loud and very repetitive method of guilt, shame and condemnation. His voice will often bring about confusion, doubt, discouragement and destruction. His voice lures me away from a life of God.

There is a difference between condemnation and conviction. Condemnation will always lead to self. It could be guilt of self, shame, selfish ambition, avoidance, isolation or destruction. Whereas, conviction will always restore you back to relationship with Jesus. It will bring about humility, restoration, truth and healing.

Often, our thoughts are affected by our likes and dislikes in life. Our fault comes when we place our intentions first and confuse them with God's voice. I learned early on, whether that a pastor or another person speaking a word of God over my life, I want to always double check a spoken word of encouragement with the written word of God. I sit before the Lord and meditate on His truth. Again, any word whether I think it or someone else speaks it, should align with the truth of His written word. We are all human and sometimes fall short of interpreting God's voice.

We certainly have tools to increase our discernment. The more time we spend seeking the heart of God, the more it will connect our spirit with His. But even the enemy can use people to speak things that might target our hearts. We must test the words of others and align the words with His truth. The important thing to remember in learning the difference between our voice and God's voice is to quiet our minds. We tend to grab hold of things that seem logical, perhaps even wise, and think that it might be God speaking. I believe God speaks to our hearts. Therefore, we need to silent those rampant thoughts whirling in our minds and allow God to speak to the heart of our spirits. God's voice will have a much bigger picture outside of our view point. Though our minds were brilliantly created, we have limitations. His voice is always perfect. His timing is perfect and His communication is perfect.

Distinguishing between His voice and our voice can also be determined by the character of God produced in and through us. We have to ask, does it boost my ego and desires? Does it exalt Jesus? We should question the position of our hearts. Am I in a place of seeking the Lord? Am I in a place of self? Is my desire to trust and walk in obedience, or is my desire to get what I want and do what I want? We must examine our heart.

Finally, I believe that we often hear His voice, but our emotions tend to be the last in line to follow. I know there have been several times in my life that I heard God's voice, but my heart was not aligned with what He was telling me. I either denied and refused it or simply was too hurt to receive it. I found it absolutely necessary to agree with the truth, act on His truth and immediately be obedient to what He was speaking to me, regardless of my emotions. My first example was forgiveness. The Lord spoke to my heart about forgiveness and my emotions did not want to parallel with what He was speaking to me. I had a choice. I could recognize that the enemy often uses our emotions to keep us in bondage, or I could respond to God immediately and walk in His truth despite my emotions. I soon comprehended the amount of freedom and reward I obtained by trusting God. I was not allowing the emotions to dictate my path, rather God's truth to guide my path. This is not an easy road, but a much advised road. It doesn't mean to suppress emotions, rather not allow emotions to overrule what God wants to do in our lives.

CHAPTER 5

HEAVENLY WORSHIP

After six months of learning, I began to hear and know God's voice. Learning His voice was choosing to enter into His presence. It was in His presence that things changed in my life. It was devoted time working through the lies that once held strongholds in my mind and heart. It was learning His voice and His power through the moments of tearing down all of my preconceived ideas and developed self- perceptions. I had worked through countless tears of anguish from previous years of abuse that once held me in silence. I worked through some of the disappointments I had in God. I didn't understand why He had allowed so much criticism, neglect and abuse to continue on in my life. His voice began to penetrate through the darkness and bring healing into the secret places deep within my heart. His voice of truth pierced the issues that once left me abandoned, rejected and falsely accused by the very people who once claimed to love me. He began to reveal the reasons I refused to believe God and to trust Christians. I learned to hear His voice through months of getting to intimately know His heart for me. I learned His voice through my quiet times, through my hours of journaling and through my moments hiking. I was relating to God, and allowing God to relate to me. I would stop and listen to His voice while worshipping, or reading His word and in prayer. I silenced my thoughts and spent my hours meditating on truth. I was waiting on Him and seeking Him with all my heart. I would enjoy secluding myself to seek more of Him and

His heart. I wanted more, sought more and He began to open new chapters in my life. It was through this tearing down process that He began to restore and build me up again.

Choir of Angels

One day I was sitting, praying and asking the Lord to speak to me, when it seemed my spiritual eyes had been opened. I saw before me intense blinding bright light. I was suddenly aware that my ears seemed to be attentive to these voices singing off in a distance. I could not figure out what was happening. I opened my eyes from prayer and checked to see if my stereo was on. I realized forgetting I was in my room that did not even contain a stereo. I laid down on my bed and continued seeking the Lord. The picture was the same luminous light, but the singing was amplified. This time I began to hear something astounding. It seemed like a multitude of voices worshipping. It was overwhelming, with a presence that penetrated deep into my heart. I had chills down my entire body listening to the voices sing echoing over what seemed the entire universe. It was captivating, leaving me in amazement of the rich and reverberating music. It was beautiful harmony. As I stood in place, my life seemed to stand still for a moment in time. I could not see where these sounds were coming from, but I had no doubt who it was coming from. It was not possible for any human or even a large choir to coordinate such elegance and power in unison. It was the most beautiful synchronization of voices. It was booming in one accord, with one purpose, and that was worship. For a brief moment in my life, my ears were opened to hear the most astonishing sound of all. It was a multitude of angels singing praises to our King. It was a piece of heaven that I was able to grab a hold of in my spirit. I look forward to the day when I too get to join in with the angels, and bow before the Lord and worship Him. This was the beginning of the Lord using visions and prophecy to bring healing, hope and anticipation of Him. It was an unforgettable moment. It demonstrated the power of prayer, transform into a priceless vision of Heaven. This experience encouraged me into a personal healing journey. I realized the more I cultivate an attitude of worship, and invite the presence of the Lord; I could experience God in a powerful way.

Then I looked and heard the voice of many angels, numbering thousands upon thousands, and ten thousand times ten thousand. They encircled the throne and the living creatures and the elders. (Revelation 5:11)

CHAPTER 6

JESUS WEPT OVER ME

It was a morning I will never forget. It was a day that forever changed my life and how I would live my life. I awoke from a terrible presence. It truly felt as if I had been raped in the midst of my sleep. I arose, feeling a presence on top of me. It was accompanied by severe cramps, stomach pain and a feeling of disgust. This was not the first time, and it seemed if I did not confide in somebody it would not be the last. I immediately called a friend. She was my prayer warrior. As I told her what happened, I could quickly detect some hesitation in her voice. She said, "The Lord has been putting things on my heart for awhile now. I have listened intently to your story, and this is bringing confirmation to what the Lord has been showing me." I was surprised, yet somewhat relieved. I was insistent to know what the Lord was placing on her heart. I asked, "What has God been showing you?" I was frightened and curious at the same time. Her response was predictable. She calmly spoke saying, "You need to allow the Lord to speak to your heart. Sit in His presence and wait on Him. Ask the Lord what He wants to reveal to you." Then she continued to say, "It is important for the Lord to show you things, therefore nothing will be wrongfully implanted into your mind." I fell silent over the phone. I knew the wisdom she was imparting was true and vital for my healing process. I agreed and decided my next step was to end the conversation in prayer. I hung up the phone and immediately sought the Lord for truth. I surrendered my own thoughts, and my life to prepare for what He was going to reveal in my heart. I was reassured that whatever the Lord would show me, it would be for my benefit. I knew I could get through it with the Lord's help.

I am a person that loves to sit on the swings and be lulled to relaxation. I was headed exactly in that direction. I was going to pray, while I listened to some worship music and simply ask the Lord to expose the hidden things in my heart. It was nearly a mile walk to the desired swings. They were located in a small tranquil park next to some mature landscape and a stream with a quiet, captivating current. It was a place that I often would hear God's voice. I turned the volume of my music to a soft hum, while I continued walking down the path. I quietly asked the Lord, "What do you want to show me?" I quickly heard a whisper of love in my heart. His voice left me with five words, echoing my achy heart. In disbelief, I laughed ignoring the possibility of horrifying truth. My thoughts swirled within; I must not be hearing His voice. So, this time I turned off my music and once again prayed seeking to hear the Lord. I asked, "Father what you want me to hear today?" The reply was consistent and I panicked. I reassured myself, this is not true. I continued walking closer to my desired destination, when I asked for the third time. "Lord, help me silent my thoughts. Help me clearly understand your heart, and your voice. What do you want to reveal to me? Lord, I desire truth and to hear your heart." I prayed against any plans of the enemy to confuse me. I prayed the Lord would silence the voice of my enemy. "Lord, will you show me what you want me to hear?" This time he spoke directly to my heart. This time, it stopped me in my tracks. I was within 50 feet of the swings, standing in the middle of the sidewalk. A vision, clearer than anything before appeared in my sight. It pierced my heart and spirit. There was Jesus with His hands on His knees, bent over gasping for air. He turned His face toward me with tears streaming down His face. He began speaking with agony in His voice, almost as if it took everything within Him to speak to me. He spoke the very same five words I was trying so hard to avoid. He said, "Satanic ritual abuse, sacrifice and slavery." My life paused before me. Instantaneously, memories flashed before my eyes. I was paralyzed with agony that was once forgotten. This brief moment in time, confirmed a bewildered, and lost childhood. The Lord's voice became a soft echo amongst the rising pain.

I stood, feeling tears well-up in my eyes until they overflowed down my cheeks. Everything within me wanted to refute what He was showing me. Yet everything within me seemed to piece together the terror of my past. The demoralizing words, the panic, the heart stopping, shrilling fragments seemed to come together in my mind. A familiar pattern of denial emerged back into reality.

I sprinted back home without missing a step. I burst into the house hunting for the phone. Where did I put it? My mind was in a mode of crisis, a mode which I was very familiar with. I was gasping for air, dismissing the fatigue from the mile I just sprinted. I was intent on finding the phone. Panic surged in me, as if I was suddenly aware of all the fear I had once forgotten. I was once again sensitive to the spiritual realm that once haunted and tormented me. Finally, I found the phone. Immediately I hit redial. My friend answered, and I persisted for an answer. I asked, "What was God showing you?" She refused to answer, recognizing the turmoil in my voice. She asked, "Are you okay?" I responded with a shrewd answer, "No, I am not okay. I think the Lord showed me what He wants to expose in my heart." With a quick, but quiet tenderness, she responded and said, "Okay." I said, "You know, don't you?" Again, with a caring voice she said, "I believe the Lord gave me three things. However, I don't want to speak first. I want to bring you confirmation, rather than information." I said, "This is what I heard." I shared the five words the Lord spoke to me, and then told her the vision I saw. I wanted to deny everything. I was desperately hoping to be wrong. Nevertheless, that wasn't the case. It was quiet for awhile. Finally, I broke the stillness over the phone. I asked, "Are you still there?" She said, "Yes, I am here." Fighting tears, my voice began to shake with the possibility of a harsh reality. I softly questioned, "Am I wrong? Please tell me I am wrong." I was almost begging to be wrong. Conversely, I knew there was too much evidence, to be wrong. I was nearly in tears with a whirlwind of thoughts and no doubt intense emotions resurrecting within me. Conflict consumed me. I waited for her response. The lack of her voice seemed to bring enough confirmation in my heart. Yet I held to a silent and prolonged hope. I asked again, "Is this true? Please tell me this is not happening to me." She responded saying, "Those were the exact same words the Lord spoke to me." The compassion in her voice attempted to soothe my heart. Yet it failed. She said, "I have been praying for you. I did not want to have to tell you. I knew only the Lord would know how to speak to your heart. I don't want this to be true for you, but God has been showing me for a month now, of things that He wants to deliver you from and this is the start of a journey in uncharted waters." My heart instantly broke. I trusted God and I sought him, three different times and I heard His voice, and I had a very clear picture. This was a road I knew would go deep into the pain of my heart. I needed to know the truth and have specific confirmation outside of myself.

Sources of Confirmation

When all this began to unfold and the Lord clearly showed me the five life changing words, I was encouraged to seek out confirmation. I was instructed to search for a high school friend, church member, sibling, counselor or any family member that would be able to give me some insight. Of course, I was no longer in contact with high school friends, or former church members. My brother condemned me for decisions made in the past. Lastly, all my family members who were safe for me were rarely around my home while growing up. So, it left me to seek the truth in Jesus Christ through avenues of His written and spoken word. I also consulted with a trusted counselor. She had worked with me for several years. Finally, I discussed some family history, patterns and behaviors that were noticeable to relatives who were around my home on occasions while growing up.

In my alone time, I sought answers to find order both in my mind and heart. At the same time, I was involved and dedicated to a group Bible study. My revelation of my past occurred simultaneously with the lessons planned in our guided schedule. It was not a coincidence what God wanted to uncover that week. Our group lesson led me to the passage of scripture in the Old Testament. It scripture was; He *burned sacrifices in the Valley of Ben Hindnom and sacrificed his sons in the fire, following the detestable ways of the nations of the Lord had driven out before the Israelites."* (2 Chronicles 28:3) This verse caught my attention. After Bible study I went back home to pray. I said to the Lord, "I need more confirmation. I have to know truth." It became my soul desire, good or bad, to find the facts of my past. My body, mind and my heart told me this is all true, but I wrestled believing this unfathomable pain of torture, hatred and betrayal was real. I battled the reality of faint memories with the denial of unwanted pain. I found myself before the Lord desperately seeking anything to refute the evidence. Regardless of the outcome, I knew I needed to press on. For many days, even months, my journey altered from denial to pain. I varied from tears to anger, acceptance and denunciation. I lost my grip to hang onto what I knew and surrendered it to what God wanted me to know. It was a journey to place my hand in His hand. It was a point that I simply said to the Lord, "I will trust you." I began turning to scriptures in the Bible. I felt the presence of the Holy Spirit guide me. *But when he, the Spirit of truth, comes, he will guide you into all truth.* (*John 16:13*) I felt the Lord led me to the next passage. *"They have built the high places of Baal to burn their sons in the fire as offerings to Baal—something I did not command or mention, nor did it enter my mind. Vs. 6; so beware, the days are coming, declares the Lord, when people will no longer call this place Topeth or the Valley of Hinnon, but the Valley of Slaughter."(Jeremiah19:5)* Then the Lord led me directly to the next scripture;. *"You will burn with lust among the oaks and under every spreading tree; you sacrifice your children in ravines and under the overhanging crags." (Isaiah 57:5)* Finally, He revealed His message; And *you took your sons and daughters whom you bore to me and sacrificed them as food to the idols. Was your prostitution not enough? Vs. 21 You slaughtered my children and sacrificed them to the idols." (Ezekiel 16:20&21)* I knew I wasn't stumbling onto these without purpose. I had never read these passages prior to this moment. I was seeking the Lord in prayer. I submitted to whatever He wanted to show me. I didn't want this to be true. I was stunned. I was shocked. How can this be real? I knew that in some odd way it brought about answers and a confirmation in my heart. It was as if my mind was thinking, I have been trying to tell you this for years. Finally you are listening to me. My mind was also torn thinking, this can't be happening to me! How do I know this isn't the power and suggestion of my mind? I refuse to believe it. I simply refuse it. Yet the conflict arose within. There were too many red flags in my past to deny the possibility of exactly what God was trying to make known. Therefore, I found myself wanting to know more.

The pieces of the puzzle were tightly fitting into place, creating the bigger picture. I always struggled trusting. I had tremendous fears.

I was diagnosed with severe PTSD, anxiety and depression. I wrestled with eating disorders, suicide, and homosexuality. There had to be something in my past to create such a distressed life. I rarely felt peace in my mind. I battled thoughts of being crazy, hearing voices and never understanding what was going on in my mind. I had piercing and unexplainable body pains. I rarely slept. The rare nights I did sleep, it was often accompanied by terrifying and helpless dreams. I frequently found myself in a "fight or flight" response. These were only a few pieces clarifying the confusion in my mind. Other memories would come and go like mighty waves, rushing in the reminders of my past.

I knew there were a few foundations I could stand on. I believed in the strong relationship I had developed over the last six months with Jesus. I knew despite my emotional highs and lows, I could stand on His infallible truth. Even though hearing His voice can sometimes be miscued by the "human element", I had learned to seek Him and align His spoken word with His written word. I can stand on His word; says, *"Whether you turn to the right or the left, your ears will hear a voice behind you saying, "This is the way; walk in it". Vs 30The Lord will cause you to hear his majestic voice. (Isaiah 30:21&31)*I applied cultivating His presence. I waited on Him, seeking His truth knowing whatever lied ahead, He can set me free. *"Then you will know the truth, and the truth will set you free". (John 8:32)*

I questioned the Lord: what else? How can I gain truth about this matter? I don't want to make things up, but I don't want to deny the evidence and facts that have been laid out directly and intentionally before me. I felt very fortunate that the woman that had been counseling me had over ten years of experience working with women overcoming trauma in their lives. Therefore, her advice was priceless as the shock factor began to settle in my mind.

Her advice was to not search every internet website on the matter. She did not want me to collect information that may not apply to me. I carefully heeded her wisdom. I did not want to be reckless in searching for wisdom and understanding. So, in order to not have ideas suggested or implanted in my mind through random websites, I turned to God's truth for answers. When this all became evident and pieces of the puzzle were taking shape, it was His truth that brought forth confirmation. Following time spent with the Lord, moments of verification emerged from other resources. Counselors, friends, relatives, doctors and intercessors had indisputable evidence of substantiation. I sought God first, and then came an abundance of proof through trustworthy people.

I continued to seek the Lord in His word, in prayer and waiting. It was not a coincidence when people in my life, that did not know what my situation was, began to surface. I received emails, stating, I do not know what is going on in your life, but the Lord has placed you on my heart. Many conversations were very specific words spoken to me, strongly indicated I was on the right path. These women were God-fearing women that were obedient to the Lord. They shared what was on their heart, without knowing what was on mine. God supernaturally brought confirmation through these women sharing their hearts with me. I was grateful to have them in prayer over me, and was thankful God used them to continue pouring out words of confirmation.

I sought truth in resources I knew were reliable, professional and trustworthy. I contacted a former counselor, and began to ask her questions about my previous sessions with her. I was looking for any evidence that may dispute what God was showing me. I was in denial and wanted reason to stay there. After three years of counseling with her, we were only able to scratch the surface of the problematic areas in my life. My anxiety, denial and other areas of my life overwhelmed my counseling time with her. Therefore, I suppressed issues that were surfacing again in my life. I knew the relationship was a strong baseline of support. I trusted, valued and respected her professional credentials, capability and relationship with Christ. I knew her insight would be invaluable. Initially I called and left a message, giving her some details of God's revelation in my life. She returned my phone call within days. My heart began racing with the uncertain outcome. Our conversation was straight forward.

I described the nightmares, visions, body pains, and memories. She became more inquisitive. I answered each question with honesty and the reality of unbearable truth. My personal file was either nearby or in her hand. The information once used in my counseling, brought confirmation to my exposed pain. Results from written tests and analysis, professional diagnosis, and years of counseling were the forefront of the battle now invading my life. It was strongly apparent denial was not an option anymore. I crumbled after our phone conversation. I knew I had ample time to understand God's direction in my life. It was frightening. My life would surely be different from this point forward. I had numerous occasions of confirmation. I had several words and pictures from the Lord. I studied Psychology in college and even found a section on the effects of ritual abuse. Speaking to my counselor sealed the deal. It was time to trust God and move forward in His leading.

CHAPTER 7

THE LION AND THE LAMB

Regardless of my age, I often found myself pondering a few issues that seemed to bring confusion and very few answers. In my life those issues stemmed from two questions. What is love and who am I? I assumed most people knew what love was, and it certainly appeared people were certain of who they were and what their "purpose" was in life. Perhaps, it was a misconception on my part, or a harsh reality for me. Either way, I viewed others knowing their reason, or identity in life and being fulfilled in relationships. I, on the other hand felt I was observing life from the outside. I was the one, who never experienced enough trust to build healthy, strong relationships. I was not confident in my purpose or love. I often dwelled on my shortcomings and felt the inner chaos brought a lot of confusion. This journey I begun required answers. Would I grasp who I really was? Would I really know love?

Most weeks, it seemed there were multiple times that I would be triggered. In the beginning, I wouldn't even recognize a trigger, until my emotions were escalated and overwhelming. Triggers are present day events that cause an emotional over-response from a past traumatized episode. An example might be a loud unexpected balloon popping that initiates a memory of a gun releasing in a traumatic circumstance. My only way out of these episodes of panic and anguish was to have some one walk me through the emotional state of crisis. That task came down to one strong woman. She did not fully comprehend the extent of my past, but she was able to understand the approach to my healing through her own personal story of pain. She knew the difficulty of overcoming pain and crisis in her own life. Therefore she was perfectly suited to help me through my journey.

Although betrayal was not a driving force in her own life, it certainly dictated the thoughts and decisions in my life. Betrayal haunted every footstep in life, and I felt I would never be free from people who strongly damaged my heart through betrayal. From childhood through adulthood, even in ministry, it seemed to follow my footsteps on every path of life. It is understandable we have all suffered from a family member or a friend betraying us. After all, we do live in a fallen world. However, this kind of betrayal I battled was seeded deep in my heart and as I stated earlier, it impacted me for a lifetime.

Triggers were frequently occurring, and emotional pain was undeniable. It was certain God was exposing the dark secrets hidden in my heart. I prayed routinely for God to expose the buried pain in my heart. God's answer in prayer certainly does not always present itself in the manner we wish. However, He is good to remove the unwanted areas in our lives in order to produce good fruit. *He cuts off every branch in me that bears no fruit, while every branch that does bear fruit He prunes so that it will be even more fruitful. (John 15:2)* I wanted God to remove anything that would hinder me from truly and intimately experiencing His love. I wanted to know His love. I felt, if I could have the lies and pain removed, it would be possible for me to grasp His love. He was very faithful every time to bring some unwanted lies, attitudes and false belief systems to the surface. He would show memories hidden in the past that needed to be exposed. This time was no different. The pain of betrayal surfaced. The familiar feelings paralyzed me. I would not intentionally subject myself to betrayal, it would randomly trigger me. My response resulted in isolation, independence, and a lack of trust with people and God.

I would guard my heart and vow never to trust. I would lash out in frustration and attempt to abandon God. My mind was determined to "do it myself" and never depend on anyone. I would agree with the lies swirling in my mind. It would create panic and an emotional response that was a foreboding road. This trigger continued to escalate until I had little balance inside my mind. It was at that point, I knew if I didn't call out for help, these triggers would result in something terrible.

After calming down, I reasoned through the triggers. I recognized God exposing this deep rooted area of my life. Therefore, I refused to abandon God, rather respond opposite of my feelings. I needed to trust God in this journey. Despite of the real emotions and pain, God was beckoning me to walk with Him. I needed freedom and healing. The only way out of the captivity of betrayal was holding His hand. I knew this was a vital week of counseling. Every week seemed crucial, but some weeks my life depended on His miracles. I made my way down to my second home and found shelter, rest, comfort and usually some chocolate too.

The next morning I awoke and we began our day of prayer. Our prayer and counseling sessions varied according to the specific areas God wanted to work on. My friend and I worked as a team. Our foundation was to follow the Lord. Every session we invited the Holy Spirit to be our counselor. *And I will ask the Father, and He will give you another Counselor to be with you forever—the Spirit of truth. (John 14:17)* We would plead the blood of Jesus over the house in protection. In the power and authority that is in Christ Jesus, we rebuked and silenced the voice and plans of the enemy. We would each submit our hearts, lives, assets and loved ones to Him. We gave God permission to work in each of our lives. We broke agreement with lies, vows, covenants, and anything else that hindered us from receiving from Him. We prayed for divine wisdom, insight, revelation, and discernment. We remained humble, knowing only the true Jesus could deliver me and set me free. With our hearts humbled in prayer, God quickly prompted areas in my heart where He wanted freedom.

This week it was pinpointing the specific area of betrayal. Within moments a strong panic attack hit me. I felt as though I could not breathe. I felt like sobbing, but knew it would be difficult to get any air if I was crying. I felt chilled down to my bones, and nothing was able to keep me warm. My friend placed several blankets over me in hopes that would help. I recognized the cold must be a memory surfacing. Memories can be stored in the mind and the body. My body and mind felt trapped.

I had clear images of horrifying pictures from my past. I was a young child, probably around the age of 7. I saw myself standing close to a swiftly moving stream. The streamed carved a twisted path through the wooded area nearby my house. It flowed alongside a small single track trail which led to the isolated quarry. Next to the quarry3 set the town's cemetery, a local trash dump, and densely wooded acreage eventually leading to unoccupied farmland. Although, I sat in the safety of a nice home and a wonderful friend, the reality was like I was in that familiar place of horror. My head ached as the memories emerged and my heart agonized over the reality of the pain surfacing. My body and mind wanted freedom from the pain trapped inside. My mind was speaking as though I was reliving the trauma. Terror gripped me as I began to work through the panic of the memories. I began to describe the unfolding horror. I was centered on a jagged boulder next to the stream, hidden in the woods. My screams were assuredly silenced by the canopy of the towering trees, and the rush of the water flowing. I stood shivering on the rock that seemed to represent an alter. I did not have many clothes covering me, rather just the basic necessities hanging from my chilled body. I was crying and scared as it appeared that there were three adult figures in front of me. Although I was not able to clearly distinguish their faces, I knew that two of them were my parents. In the memory I could easily recognize the voices, body shapes and even familiar agendas.

It was a ritualistic punishment stricken upon my spirit, body and mind. It was a wicked and evil force placed on me. Perhaps the punishment was for failing to be obedient to my father. Possibly it was a form of torture, like many rituals, undeserved and only served as a wretched injustice to gain their agenda. Their agendas could serve many purposes. Maybe it was to shape me to become a servant of evil, or manipulate me to become their own slaves. Perhaps it was to simply turn me completely from the true Jesus. Ideally, their bottom line was to belittle my-self worth, voice, identity, relationships and future that would exist outside their control. I was broken in order to understand "their power" was greater than God and me. I was deceived, beaten and nearly killed, in order to comprehend the jurisdiction I served would haunt me forever if I don't obey. They made every bruise; torturous act and manipulative word command my every thought and decisions. Their agendas were to control, overpower and destroy me. Their plans began at a young age for me. Their evil intentions were already in motion by the time I was seven.

As we continued our session, the memory brought more clarity. Lying on the comfy couch, layered with blankets, my body trembled with the next images coming to my mind. I was quivering from the memory of the night air. It was dark and frightening. I felt a twinge down my body. I stood paralyzed and crying. The soft tingling sensation grew into horrifying realities. My eyes that were once closed, opened to the terror of spiders crawling up and down my bare body. I screamed while my parents watched the "show" unfold. I was helpless and terrified. I saw the spiders grow in numbers. I felt two or three. Then it became ten or more. They ran across the front and back of me. Fear surged through my mind and body. I sensed it once again; I jumped up off the couch and yelled, "Get them off me". As an adult, the memory was simply too real to deny the sensation of my past. It was horrifying. Calming down and sitting back on the couch, I knew the memory was only the beginning of the problematic areas I needed to work through. I took a deep sigh and allowed the remaining portions of the memory to ascend. I stood on a fashioned alter with spiders crawling all over me. Those who I trusted the most, and needed their help, watched me slowly deteriorate in sheer terror. It was exactly what they wanted, and it didn't stop there. It was a confusing message that was meant to be carved in my heart for the rest of my life. With force, they grabbed me by my arm pulling me down from the large boulder. They brushed every harmless yet terrifying spider off me, and drug me to a tragic view of the next dreadful act. I collapsed in sorrow and grief, as I clearly saw a small constructed grave site ahead of my footsteps. Refusing every step, the force grew more demanding and my weak framed body submitted to the overpowering grip on my arms. Pushed into the small wooden box, I laid there crying as I watched my trusted parents shovel cold lifeless dirt over my quivering and frightened body. I was speechless and helpless as the suffocating soil weighed me down. My head remained uncovered, but my body was shamefully buried. Nothing remained in me. Betrayal pierced deep in my heart and would remain there only growing in depth and anger. I experienced an ultimate hurt that no child or living creature should ever have to endure. Although I was allowed the privilege to breathe, my heart desired to die. My parents then exalted themselves as the hero. They rescued me from the pit, in which I would always be grateful of their kindness. In return, it would teach me the conflicting idea of power, obedience and submission. It also instilled the perplexing message of God's deliverance, helplessness, fear, betrayal and a strong misjudgment of who I should trust.

Prayer was never meant to unfold the stories of my past so that I could harbor anger, unforgiveness and resentment. Healing can allow opportunities of the past to surface only when countering the past with truth and life. Forgiveness and repentance are a conduit to freedom. We are not to remain in bondage of our past, rather seek avenues of healing and truth in order to live an abundant life now. My sessions of prayer and counseling were always intended for me to face my past so that I could have a deeper understanding of my relationship with Christ and my identity in Him. I realized I often looked for an identity and belonging to a group through materialistic, natural gifts. I did not see my identity through the eyes of my personal relationship with Jesus. I did not see my value through my relationship with Jesus. I saw my value through what I could do for Jesus. There is a big difference in doing works in order to achieve an identity, compared to doing works coming from an established identity, of who I am in Christ. It was from lessons of betrayal that originally taught me to work for approval. However, it is the truth seeking journey and visions of Jesus that brought the deep healing in my heart. It was images of my worth in Jesus that freed me from the bondage of betrayal.

After revisiting the memory, there was a good portion of the day left to allow Jesus to minister His truth and healing in my life. We were still before God waiting and listening to what He wanted to speak. We both knew this was only scraping the surface of the issue of betrayal in my life. I knew His truth could dismantle the web of lies I had believed and experienced over time. We quietly invited the Holy Spirit to speak and minister to these areas of my heart. In a short time, the Lord placed me back in the same memory. This time, I was not trembling, but could feel the fear. The feelings were not overwhelming as before, but I was still uneasy with the surroundings I saw in my mind. I could see where I was standing, and felt a coolness come over my cheeks. I waited, praying for the Lord to deliver me from evil and come and rescue me. *Even though I walk through the valley of the shadow of death, I will fear no evil, for you are with me; your rod and staff comfort me. (Psalm 23:4)* I surveyed my surroundings and saw the same large, strong trees nearby. It seemed as if I could see the evil presence lurking above. There was no doubt the presence of demons had joined in the ritual acts with the intentions to gain evil power. It was as if I could hear the screeching and drooling of evil above me. I prayed again for the Lord to come quickly and rescue me. I sincerely wrestled with forgiveness. I insisted my parents did not deserve forgiveness, but realized I deserved the freedom that came from forgiveness. I reluctantly but sincerely forgave those who inflicted pain upon me. I broke agreement with the plans of the enemy and the evil spirits of darkness. I quickly aligned myself with the Kingdom of the Most High God. I renounced any vows I was forced to make with my parents and with the ritual acts. I agreed to follow the plans of the True Lord Jesus and His Kingdom of Light. I bound my mind, body and spirit with the True Jesus. In an instant, I saw before me a dark shadow slowly begin to appear. It was unusual, because though I was surrounded by evil, this shadow did not seem to frighten me. In fact it sparked a curiosity. I squinted my eyes in search of this creature coming closer to me. Then I began to see the body take shape. A lion, strong in stature stood before me. He had chains of bondage laced around His front paws. He sat down with His hind legs slightly bent, in order for Him to posture Himself upright. With a great roar, His mouth expanded and His teeth exposed. Then, I witnessed the deliverance from evil. Every creepy, slimy, dark, deceitful, evil creature quickly vanished. They could not handle being in the presence of this mighty Lion. My eyes refocused on this intriguing Lion. He stood on all four legs. His legs rippled a mighty strength. His straightforward chest presented righteousness. His mane radiated safety and peace. As His front paws shook the ground beneath. The thick chains splintered in half. The chains could not hold Him. He stepped forth with a vengeance and passion. His presence emerged from this dark landscape and I was able to clearly see in His eyes. His eyes were colorfully filled with love and justice. I began to weaken and slowly weep as I stared into His merciful, golden eyes. It was not the color of His eyes that captivated me. It was the compassion that overflowed from His eyes. I stood amazed. His eyes seemed to bring forth restoration, judgment and peace all in one. Yet, I knew the judgment was not cast upon me, but upon the place I stood and the evil afflicted on me. I stood in awe of this magnificent and ferocious Lion. I realized He was not here to devour me, but to free me. He was the Lion of Judah. It was the Lion that triumphed over the darkness. *See, the Lion of the tribe of Judah, the Root of David, has triumphed. He is able to open the scroll and its seven seals. Then I saw a Lamb, looking as if it had been slain, standing in the center of the throne, encircled by the four living creatures and the elders. (Revelation 5:5)* At this time, I realized I did not feel fearful and helpless. Instead, I felt empowered and free. I began to have hope. At that moment, when the Lion was easing His way closer to me, I noticed a Lamb also followed him. It was a small Lamb. Joy transpired from my spirit, and there was something special and captivating about this Lamb. In this vision, the presence of the Lamb enveloped me, supernaturally removing my pain and sorrow. The tenderness of this Lamb exchanged my anguish for His joy. The transformation was mind boggling. I was being moved from fear to faith. I was experiencing the transition from darkness to light. I witnessed the presence of evil to the glorifying and redeeming presence of life. It was powerful and miraculous. How could a life filled with betrayal witness such a spiritual effect that would drastically change my natural mind? It was truly encountering the presence of Christ. He was removing me from the past and placing new things before me. *Forget the former things; do not dwell in the past. See, I am doing a new thing! Now it springs up' do you not perceive it? I am making a way in the desert and streams in the wasteland. (Isaiah 43:18 &19)* I was being redeemed by the blood of the Lamb. I thought this was magnificent and knew it would be difficult to describe, but the unveiling picture was not finished. The Lion and the Lamb were next to me. Then something even greater appeared before me. It was a figure of a man. The shadows faded as the light outlined His presence. Where He stood darkness fled. There was a sharp and distinguished separation between Him and the backdrop of darkness. The distant darkness resembled the shattered past. His light overpowered and severed the darkness. He slowly walked toward me and a peace filled me. The betrayal of my childhood slowly seemed to slip away. The fear, aggression and pain of betrayal no longer held me in the confinement of my past. I was beginning to experience a new level of freedom that I never thought would happen. I had no doubt I was encountering the presence of the True Lord Jesus. There was a very distinct clarity in my spirit. Jesus knelt down before me, and with His eyes alone asked for permission to pick me up. I was enthralled with His presence. We did not have to verbally communicate. Our spirits became one. We communicated in our spirit. With His arms outstretched, He lifted me up. I placed my hands on His shoulders and we embraced. I began to notice that the sleeve of His garment clothed my once bare body. I found myself clothed in royalty. The robes draped to my feet and the feeling of a soft velvety robe colored in deep purple clothed me as a child of His inheritance. Instantaneously, I was dressed. The nakedness of my past was now covered in the promises of my Savior. *Later I passed by, and when I looked at you and saw that you were old enough for love, I spread the corner of my garment over you and covered your nakedness. I gave you my solemn oath and entered into a covenant with you, declares the Sovereign Lord, and you became mine. (Ezekiel 16:8)* In a divine supernatural moment, the shame of my past was exchanged for a garment of royalty. In that moment I realized He was saying to me, I was His. My value of life evolved from the knowledge of intimacy with Christ.

I began the prayer session questioning love, and specifically His love for me. I wondered, what was my identity and the purpose of my life? Though it came through suffering, it was in the light of His glory that He began to answer those life-long questions.

My brokenness of betrayal was fading, as I broke the agreement of lies I believed. My next steps were to repent of the lies I believed, and forgive those who taught me the pain of betrayal. I entrusted the Lord with my pain. I allowed those moments of agony to overflow into sobs. I invited Jesus to be present in my condition, healing the scars and voids once occupied by deep pains of my heart. His Holy Spirit felt like a gentle ray of sunlight, warming my spirit. I quietly rested in the comfort of His presence. I was beginning to feel a soothing sense of love. I was able to receive a gift of affirmation, knowing it was unconditional. This welcomed sensation dissipated my fears. My darkness was exchanged for light, and my spirit transitioned into joy.

As I waited upon the Lord, He displayed truth in images I was able to understand. He showed me, that my identity was developed from the "earthly tasks" I performed in order to receive love and acceptance. I received my identity first through talents. I tired of the efforts I made to "belong" in a group. I selfishly pursued ambitions in order for me to find my place in this world. My reasons, though valid, stemmed from betrayal. The absence of security I encountered through relationships of people I should have been able to trust led me to a road of false identity. I felt I needed to "work" for my security, identity and purpose in life. However, the Lord was showing me exactly the opposite. He gave me a picture of three boxes. They were like the Russian babushka dolls, all a different size, with the smallest box in the center or core of the other two boxes. I opened the first box and written inside were the words; passion and dreams. I opened the second box and saw the words; spiritual gifts. Lastly, I opened the third and smallest box and saw the words: relationships, identity and signet ring. The third box was the center core of the other two boxes. I asked the Lord what this meant. He showed me a ring on my finger. It was a signet ring, and He was placing it on my finger. The signet ring in the Bible represents pleasure, approval, acceptance, royal kingship, authority, love, a sealing of ownership, a king's seal representing the transferring or sharing of a royal authority. He began to speak to my heart. My identity will be known through relationship in Him, not out of works or things of this world. The security and identity established in this world will be empty. My identity flowing from a relationship with Him was the core, intimate box He gave me. I realized this box represented the core of my spirit, body and mind. My identity came from Him alone. Out of the core relationship and identity in Christ blossomed the gifts and talents He was fanning into flame. Thirdly, out of the relationship and gifts would blossom passions and dreams. Embracing His love allowed me the opportunity to understand the significance of receiving my value, through relationship in Jesus Christ. I was able to embrace His love, through the healing that was taking place in my heart. Because the truth sets you free, I was able to see things more clearly. *Then you will know the truth, and the truth will set you free. (John 8:32)* I realized often in my life, I had those priorities out of order. Yet, I know God is a God of order. Therefore, I must place my value first in an intimate relationship with Him. If I could not fully trust in Him alone, then I would not trust in the plans He had for me. My foundation was to trust Him, receive His love, and then trust the great work He desired to do in and through me.

Through the suffering of my own betrayal, I was able to share in the suffering of His betrayal. It is in the shared suffering that we also share in His glory. It is in the presence of His glory that His love is revealed. *I consider that our present sufferings are not worth comparing with the glory that will be revealed in us. (Romans 8:18)* As I grew in my relationship with the Lord, so did my identity and value solidify in Him.

CHAPTER 8

FREEDOM IN FORGIVENESS

E very week I consistently attended my counseling sessions. Rarely would I miss an opportunity for healing and freedom. I knew every time I went to my sessions, I would encounter a mental and spiritual battle. However, I also knew we often ended each session with deliverance and new life. It was a welcomed encounter with Christ. This time was not much different. This session also included a physical confirmation of my memories and deliverance from the puzzling pain in my body. It was our day to meet. I sat once again on the long, comfy couch. We began our session with our usual opening prayer. It consisted of praying the blood of Jesus over all our loved ones, belongings, finances and time. We invited the Holy Spirit to be present as we waited on His leading. We gave permission for Christ to expose the areas of darkness and strongholds. We desired His truth to bring forth revelation and insight. We bound the plans and schemes of the darkness, and silenced the voice of the enemy, by the power and authority of Christ Jesus. We continued waiting and seeking His truth in silence.

Within moments, a panicked breathing began in my chest. I could not catch my breath. At the same time, I experienced moderate shocks of voltage that pierced my body, causing me to jump unexpectantly in pain. I knew this was nothing unusual, and it did not alarm me. This wasn't the first time I experienced sharp shooting pain. In fact I grew up with a lot of unexplained pain, headaches and sickness. It was rare to have any explanation for these random pains that surged my body. I began to realize these memories had been trapped inside my body. Once I gave permission for God to expose the pain of the past, both my mind and body began telling me the memory of the baffling events. I learned that our body can testify to abuse. It can hold memories of physical pain. If those memories are not fully released in healing, our bodies will continue to hold the bondage of abuse. Our muscles remember, as well as our minds. Overtime, I became more aware of the body memories. They brought forth confirmation to the mental images lying dormant in my mind.

This time, the sharp pain in my body was reminding me of a story. As the body memories began to surface, so did the horrifying visual memories. Emotions filled with anger, pain, confusion and emotional and spiritual torment began to rise up.

That perplexing memory was deep and painful. It left lifelong trauma and damages in my mind, heart and spirit. It was an intense time seeking the Lord for complete and permanent healing. Every week I depended on him to remove me from the oaths of the past abuse in order for me to walk in a freedom, filled with truth and life. This session was another needed appointment.

I remembered when I was nine years old, which co-insided with the outward pain I was beginning to manifest through self mutilation. The Lord began to show me more than 25 years later what was really going on in a secretive and suppressed world in which I lived. He began to reveal the foundation of the complete destruction of my life.

This specific memory was like most memories — a snapshot of several pictures. Most of the memories entailed visions and emotions that lined up together. The images consisted of bondage, threats, evil people, fires, sacraments and witchcraft. The mounting emotions varied in fear, betrayal, panic, helplessness and more. As I sat on the couch, I knew deep within my spirit there was more. I surrendered before the Lord with tears in my eyes. My willing spirit prayed and said, "Lord give me courage to go to the area of my life that is being held by darkness." Shortly after that; He began to give me quick, but precise snapshots of the dark abuse. This specific abuse transpired in one night of my life, but beliefs and hurt remained in my heart for many years.

Hidden in the dense and secluded wooded area, lied a reserved area. This area was a meeting ground for rituals. It consisted of a natural rock that improvised as an alter. The secretive camp also consisted of men and women circled in an occultist group. The background was darkened by the late night sky. The presence of evil was oppressing. The memory was a ritual mockery of Christ. It was meant to remove the power of God in my life. From this moment on, I would hold considerable doubts of God's power in my life. It was their intention to gain power from Satan, and use a sacrifice to diminish the power of God. The leaders used the force of threats, power, manipulation, weapons and often physical force. This was just another occasion that fear consumed me, as I was forced to submit to an evil authority.

They secured me on a human made cross, tying me to two wooden boards. They removed my clothes and spit on me. They laughed at me, and used electric cattle prods, jolting my body until it was obvious I had enough. My body collapsed on the splintering wood. They knew exactly how much torture to inflict without leaving a trace of physical evidence. Rarely did any abuse mark me. Permanent damage was invisible to the eye. It was the summoning of demonic presence, the drinking of blood from a sacrifice, the mockery of Christ and the lack of anyone rescuing me that birthed the hatred and distrust of God. When I called out for any relief, no one seemed to hear me. The overpowering abuse of ritual darkness instilled a greater fear of evil, then a fear of God. However, presently walking in truth gave way to the knowledge that the enemy was defeated by the power of the ultimate sacrifice. I knew the memories and bondage holding me in a present day pain, would soon be diminished by the ultimate power of Christ's love for me. Even though this was incredibly tough, it was also already done. Walking forward was walking into a future of freedom. There was work still to be done, because my heart was still filled with the pain. I was real with Christ. I could not pretend this was okay. I searched for real answers from the source of truth.

I cried out to God with an angered voice and a sense of injustice. "How can you let this happen? Where were you? Why didn't you answer me? Why didn't you save me?" I was angry. My willing spirit turned into the hatred I remembered. My emotions quickly turned to the injustice of my pain. Soon I realized I was living out what I learned from this memory. My heart hardened with anger. I was saying the same words I once spoke in this specific memory. I hate God and I will never trust you, Lord. You failed me. You will fail me again. I hate those who inflicted great pain upon me.

Tears filled my eyes as I surveyed the living room. My counselor sat quietly on the other side. Her spirit was submissive as she gently spoke with condolence. "I am so sorry". She added, "I don't know really what to say, other than just keep taking it to the Lord."

I began to verbalize the pain as the snapshots continued to become a present reality. I would hear screeching of a demonic power over me. My body was weary with years of burdens never released. I was angry with valid questions. I felt torn between trying to step into healing, and wanting to accuse God for not saving me.

At this point, I did not doubt the reality of this memory. I knew my body and mind was telling truth. This memory was real. My spirit brought confirmation. There was too much evidence to deny the secret rituals. It answered a lot of questions within me, but one question still remained. Where were you, God?

Without hesitation, the Lord quietly spoke to my heart. In his gentle manner, He imparted wisdom to my spirit. He said to me, "I want to speak truth to you, but you are standing in a place of darkness. Darkness does not understand light. You must be in My light in order to understand My truth." I thought to myself. Logically and scripturally, that is true. *In Him was life, and that life was the light of men. Vs 5 the light shines in the darkness, but the darkness has not understood it. (JOHN 1:4)* I found myself in a peculiar place. I wanted to stay in a place of familiarity. Even though, my familiarity was a place of darkness. I was angry and bitter at God and people. In my opinion, I was justifiably right. In my stillness, I began to understand that I must abandon my emotions and earthly knowledge, in order to seek truth and walk in His light instead. So I asked the Lord, "What shall I do in order to walk in your light?" He said, "You must forgive, repent and give me the pain." I said, "What? I cannot do that. Did you not hear or see my story? Are you kidding me? How can I forgive?" There was a quiet moment. I argued my side and justified all the reasons I should not forgive. I took a deep breath and decided to follow Christ instead of myself. My head and heart wanted to cling to my reasoning. But my spirit wanted to surrender to the Lord. I knew in my own power I could not do what He was asking of me. I prayed that He would empower and teach me to forgive, repent and give my pain to Him.

He began to show me that in order to walk in complete freedom I must know some basic truths about forgiveness. First of all, forgiveness is not based on emotions; it is based on obedience to Him. He commands us to forgive, just as He has forgiven us. *Forgive, and you will be forgiven. (Luke 6:37)* Second, when we don't walk in forgiveness, we become subject to harvesting bitterness, resentment, hatred and behaviors that will destroy a person's life. Un-forgiveness will dry up your bones, and begin to cause a spiritual death. Third, Jesus began to teach me that forgiveness is not about the other person it is about my freedom. When I forgive a person it is severing a spiritual and emotional tie of sin between me and the person that sinned against me. In other words, when I forgive I am free from the bondage of the other person. It is taking the sword of the Spirit and cutting an invisible chord of sin between two people. I am no longer spiritually tied to the sin and the other person. He was not finished teaching me about the benefits of forgiveness. He was making it clear that there is power and freedom behind forgiveness. Fourth, He showed me that forgiveness is an act based on trusting Him. Often, I believed that if I forgive a person, then it justifies their behavior and acts towards me. The Lord clearly said that is a lie from the enemy. Forgiveness is placing trust in the sovereign hands of God to judge accordingly. Forgiveness is about our relationship with the Lord. Forgiveness binds us to the heart and will of Christ. However, unforgiveness opens areas of our lives to plans of the enemy. Finally, I felt that forgiveness meant I must be in relationship with the other person. He refined my thinking on that issue. He said that I am accountable to Him and need to walk in His wisdom. There will be times He will desire to bring healing and restoration in a relationship. He will rebuild the relationship through grace, forgiveness and eventually trust. It takes two people to re-enter a relationship. By His power and love a relationship can be restored if that is His desire. However, there are times He will wisely guide us away from relationships that are unsafe to continue. He leads according to His purposes for us. I began to realize that true forgiveness was not at all what I had been taught. He was teaching me the significance of forgiveness early on in my healing, so that I would be quick to walk in forgiveness every time. I made a habit to forgive; recognizing the true, deep freedom always blossomed from forgiveness. It is vital for our life. Healing and truth entered into my spirit through the gift of forgiveness. Forgiveness is a life giving habit to develop in our spiritual walk.

It is difficult to forget memories without forgiving. When I did forgive, I also forgot the pain of my past and remembered the new truths He gave me. In order to receive healing of our past, we must enter through a heart of forgiveness, so that we can press forward to the new promises He has for our futures.

Repentance was the second insight He began to reveal to me. My question was, "Lord what did I do that would require me to repent? I was the victim, remember?" I sensed a gentle correction in my spirit. It was a quietness that stilled my heart. I knew as He began to speak to me that I needed to repent. I sought His truth. My heart melted when His still and small voice prompted me with a couple revelations. One that I needed to repent for the lies I have believed about God, others and myself. Second, I need to repent of the non-verbal vows I made to never forgive and trust. I needed to sever my mind and spirit from the damaging bondage. I needed to be removed from the criticism I held in my heart. I needed to repent of my doubt of God's redeeming power in my life. I was amazed of all the lies that entered into my heart and life through trauma. I thought I was innocent. I began to realize… He was right. I needed to break agreement with all the lies. Repentance was in my best interest. *Therefore this is what the Lord says: "If you repent, I will restore you that you may serve me; if you utter worthy, not worthless words, you will be my spokesman. Let this people turn to you, but you must not turn to them." (Jeremiah 15:19)*

I was aware that when I believed the lies, it left no room to believe the truth. If I don't believe the truth of God in my life, then I am agreeing with the plans the enemy has for me. After all, lies can develop into belief systems. If I believe lies, then I live out the condemnation of what Satan wants me to believe. If I believe in truth, then I will live out God's plans for my life. I can live in bondage or I can live in freedom. Repentance comes from the kindness of the Lord. *Or do you show contempt, tolerance and patience, not realizing that God's kindness leads you to repentance. (Romans 2:4)*

The Lord was teaching me that repentance requires a sincere heart and a faith in Christ to empower my course of a new direction. *I (Paul) have declared to both Jews and Greeks that they must turn to God in repentance and have faith in our Lord Jesus. (Acts 20:21)*

Repentance requires a humble heart of surrender unto Him. However, it also springs forth new life. *For I take no pleasure in the death of anyone, declares the Sovereign Lord. Repent and live! (Ezekiel 18:32)* A life of repentance produces a life filled with freedom and truth. Ultimately, He showed me that forgiveness and repentance are key essentials to healing.

The last lesson felt like it was the most difficult. His revelation was crucial to my next step of healing. He did not want me to carry this pain anymore. He imparted the truth that forgiveness and pain are two separate steps in healing. I believed if I forgave someone who inflicted pain on me, then I must ignore or suppress the pain still residing in my heart. It seemed impossible to make this consideration as one package. I identified the forgiveness, repentance and giving the pain to the Lord as three separate steps. It was extremely difficult to move forward and trust the Lord if I still harbored bitterness, un-forgiveness and unwilling to repent. If I had not surrendered my heart to repentance and forgiveness first, then it would be challenging to receive His truth. My hard heart denied His truth because it was occupied with the lies and resentment of my past. I previously mentioned that forgiveness is walking in obedience. Repentance is allowing God to change my course of direction. Therefore, both choices are mindful actions to align my life with God's word. However, the distress of emotional pain still remained in my heart. Since I had aligned my will with God's truth, His promises awaited to redeem my heart. I was ready to receive my freedom through His healing truth. *Then you will know the truth, and the truth shall set you free. (John 8:32)*

My question remained... Where were you God? I felt His presence assure me. I was ready to grasp His role in this suffering. His Spirit reminded me of this scripture. *'The King will reply, 'I tell you the truth, whatever you did for one of the least of these brothers of mine, you did for me.' (Matthew 25:40)* I embraced His truth. His compassion saturated my broken heart. I felt His love flood me. He understood my pain. I embraced His words in my heart. I began to envision the horror of my memory. When the memory surfaced, I saw I was not alone.

In the darkness of the chilling night, I saw the Lord's body draped over mine. The human strikes flailing against me were confronted with the barrier of Christ's body. The lashes and electrocution was first met with the sacrificial body of Christ over me. He took upon himself the same abuse. Whatever was done to me was done to Him first. The death that ensued me that night was confronted by the compassion, power and protection of Christ. I was not meant to live. By His great love, the evil punishment was minimal. He saved me. If I would have died that night, I would guess, that my eternity would have exceeded any earthly punishment I knew to that point. Without knowing Jesus Christ as my personal savior that night, I am confident Hell would have consumed me.

I realized through the suffering, God gave His life as the ultimate sacrifice thousands of years ago. I no longer have to live as a sacrifice to others. In the memory I embraced the truth of His word. *Never will I leave you; never will I forsake you. (Hebrews 13:5)* Despite the unfortunate pain, Jesus was there with me. He covered over me. Because he laid His life down that night for me, I am able to come to Him today and receive His redemptive plan for me. I learned, my cross meant to bring death to me; His cross meant to bring forth life for me.

The thief comes only to steal and kill and destroy; I have come that they may have life, and have it to the full. Vs 11 I am the good shepherd. The good shepherd lays down his life for the sheep. (John 10:10).

CHAPTER 9

COME UNTO ME

It was not uncommon to battle thoughts of the past. Many of my beliefs were built upon the secrets of my dark past. I was not nurtured into adulthood. I learned to survive until adulthood. It was my strong survival skills that masked my pain. Although I developed highly functional coping mechanisms, the counseling sessions were carefully dismantling every wall I built. Common emotions I experienced were anger, injustice and fear. Other emotions would often surface. I struggled with trust. I wrestled with identity. I often felt helpless, hopeless and overpowered. I developed a strong sense of injustice. I thought I would never see the end to my misery. I thought my life was meant to experience pain. Even though I had fun times with friends, I still had a gaping hole of depression in my heart. Every time I would work through a difficult circumstance another would surface. There was very little time to celebrate before another memory would surface. I felt tired, weary and overwhelmed. My anxiety would be off the charts. Many times I wanted to shut down. I would experience flashbacks that seemed so real. I would believe people were following me. I was unable to sleep most nights. I was frightened at every unexpected noise. I felt as if I were re-living my past.

Every small threat over my life left a lasting imprint on my mind, body and spirit. The occult would program my mind through powerful, oppressive threats. The intricate ritual acts left me powerless to make decisions, to live a "normal" life, feel safe, and dream of good things. Instead I felt isolated, crazy, stupid, and that God would never desire to give me good things.

Through my entire healing process, I would journal all my thoughts, emotions, victories and visions. Reflecting on one section in particular, I witnessed God triggering my emotions, in order for Him to bring healing. I was sixteen years old when I started to believe God would never give me good things. I felt trapped. I never thought I would escape.

It was a rude awakening. A strong and forceful hand grabbed my arm just above the elbow. Fighting back, I attempted to pull away from this man. He overpowered me. I was forced to walk with him to the unknown. Unfortunately I knew this man. I was shocked that he would be grabbing me. I thought we were friends, even family. I did not know what was going on. My heart panicked. I could only recall bits and pieces of the memory. I was thrown in the trunk of an old vehicle and taken off to some dark wooded area. It was not the same place I was use to. I did not really know where I was. I was cuffed and silenced by rope and tape. I was in and out of consciousness. It was difficult to know the reason why this was happening. Other people were around. We were all hidden by the forest of trees around. The memory was vague and a little blurry. I remember a man transferring money into the hands of my kidnapper. Everybody involved were people that I knew. I did not know what they said, but I knew in my heart, this was not good.

I remember two men drug me to the back of the woods. I cried out to God, "Help me". I did not say it out loud, because I had tape covering my mouth. I know desperation was in my eyes. I am not sure what those men saw in me that night, but I know they were paid to do a job, and they left it unfinished. A gun was held to my head and I drifted out of consciousness. My body shut down. When I woke up, I was in pain. My clothes were torn and my body felt bruised. I was thrown into a different vehicle. This time it was the bed of an old pick- up truck.

I sat in my counseling session with tear stains covering my face. My initial response was toward God. I could not understand how this abuse continued through-out my life. Is there anything good He has for me? How can I ever escape this darkness? In my heart this memory validated every emotion I was experiencing. I had no reason to trust people in my life. I understood my response to men, Christians and God. I secretly believed that they were all bad, evil, and never wanted good things for me. I was triggered at every loud and unexpected noise, because it could have been a gun that was intended to fire.

Even though there was some validity to my emotions, there was a question that remained unanswered. Does God really have good things for me? It had already been a "fight or flight" life I lived. My healing has extended for several years. I think differently than most people. I respond differently than most people. I journeyed through more difficult circumstances the most people would ever imagine. Isn't there a point in my life where God will bring me good things? Can that happen?

I closed my eyes. The tears that welled up overflowed down my face. My heart was broken. I was devastated over my life. I began to pray to the Lord. I did not have much strength in me, but I asked the Lord to minister to my heart. My thoughts drifted. I wondered where He was during the time I was in the trunk. Where was He when I was unconscious? A scripture entered in my mind. I turned to the passage in His word. *The king's command was so urgent and the furnace so hot that the flames of the fire killed the soldiers who took up Shadrach, Meshach and Abednego. And these three men, firmly tied, fell into the blazing furnace. Then Kind Nebuchadnezzar leaped to his feet in amazement and asked his advisors "Weren't there three men that we tied up and threw into the fire?" They replied, "Certainly O king." He said, "Look! I see four men walking around in the fire, unbound and unharmed, and the fourth looks like a son of the gods." Vs. 27... They saw that the fire had not harmed their bodies, nor was a hair of their heads singed; their robes were not scorched, and there was no smell of fire on them. (Daniel 3:22-25 &27)*

The king gave praise to Jesus the Son of God. The blazing furnace never harmed the three men. It gave glory to the Lord. I can only guess my life was to end that night at the hands of evil. I wondered where He was that night. He was with me. He made sure the gun did not fire. He made sure I came out alive. I closed my eyes and in the stillness of my heart, I saw a picture before me. Initially I thought it was an angel, but I believe it was the presence of Jesus. I slowly looked from the ground up concentrating on the essence of this man. His robe was piercing white. The sleeves of His garment flowed with vengeance. I sensed this strong appearance of righteousness and justice. I looked into His eyes and saw fire. It was like a sword that severed light from darkness. I was not afraid. In fact I felt safety and protection in His presence. His splendor illuminated power and authority. I realized, a day will come when the vengeance of the Lord will judge those who afflicted me. *He put on righteousness as his breastplate, and the helmet of salvation on his head; he put on the garments of vengeance and wrapped himself in zeal as in a cloak. According to what they have done, so will he repay wrath to his enemies and retribution to his foes; he will repay the islands their due. (Isaiah 59:17-18)*

I looked at Him, and my heart received His words of truth. I heard Him speak directly to me, "I will show you the depth of my heart. I will prosper you." I was honored that the Lord wants to reveal His heart to me. It has been through the course of this journey that I am learning His heart.

It is in the depths of His heart that I find peace, rest and life. It is in His heart that love abounds.

Although I do not have all the answers, I am assured that when I go to Him, He removes the heavy burdens of my past, and exchanges them for life. *Come to me, all you who are weary and burdened, and I will give you rest. Take my yoke upon you and learn from me, for I am gentle and humble in heart, and you will find rest for your souls. For my yoke is easy and my burden is light. (Matthew 11:28-30)*

CHAPTER 10

DARKNESS ALL AROUND

Three days prior to my routine prayer and counseling sessions, I awoke and already knew the day would be a challenge. I went to work with a high level of fear. The fear came from having a heightened awareness and sensitivity of the spiritual realm. I had gone through enough to realize the spiritual realm was real. Christ died for my freedom and healing. My enemy desired nothing more than death and destruction. I experienced firsthand the power of God's deliverance from evil. I knew this upcoming week would be a time in my life I needed some deliverance. I could sense darkness around me.

I walked into work early in the morning, and the wind began to increase in velocity. As I walked from the driveway into the working area, I saw a mysterious, black object cross in front of my feet. I thought it was a cat. So I peeked around the corner of the building, and did not see anything. I was baffled, but did not think much more of it. As I continued walking towards my work table, a sudden and unexpected gust of wind whirled a stack of pots, trees and other miscellaneous items to the ground. I was startled. With my heart pounding, I began to wonder what was around me. I began to consider whether or not I was alone. I took a few more steps towards the building I was working in, and felt as though someone was towering over me. I paused for a moment, taking a deep breath through my nose and exhaled. I tried to calm my uneasy stomach and the fear that seemed to flow from head to toe. With a sudden movement, I quickly turned around to see if anyone was there. No one was around. Ironically, I don't watch horror films, yet over the years of seeing horror flick commercials, I felt that I was trapped inside a suspenseful and unwanted dark movie. I knew I would not see anyone behind me, but I needed the assurance of looking. It felt so real, that it brought shivers down my back. I finally entered the building and closed the door behind me. I prayed fervently for God's protection. I also knew that God was resurrecting some darkness in my heart, in order to bring forth His light in my heart. Although I was extremely fearful, I trusted there was a plan.

I tightly closed the door behind me, as if I could lock any dark spiritual presence outside. I felt a security by locking the outside door. I walked another 5 feet away from the door, when a violent gust of wind sliced open the heavy wood door. I stood eyes wide open, paralyzed with fear. Maybe the lock did not latch. Nodding my head, I reassured myself that must have been what happened. I cautiously walked close to the door, which was slamming back and forth into the wall. I grabbed the knob, closing the door with the weight of my body. This time, I locked the door and pulled on the handle to confirm it was shut. My doubtful prayers seemed hindered by my overcoming fear. Would God really protect me this time? I had enough! I knew I had to stand in the authority of Christ Jesus. I tightened every muscle in my body, repented for my fear and rebuked every spirit of darkness and harassment to be gone. I quickly called a friend for prayer. I knew I would need a little extra reinforcement of prayer today. She assured me that she would keep me in prayer.

As I hung up the phone, the rear exit door flung open and began to thrust back and forth against the wall. I ran down the narrow aisle of the greenhouse towards the back to shut the door, when a snake alarmed me as it slithered across my path. It was not unusual for snakes and spiders to be seen in the green-house, but the timing of it all gave me chills. By that time, I had a feeling it might be a rough day. The remainder of the day continued with unusual incidents. It seemed as if there was an unwelcomed spirit lurking nearby. I was never touched or harmed. I felt the more I allowed myself to be ensnarled and consumed by its presence, the more it seemed to harass me. However, as I consistently prayed it seemed to be dismantled and its existence merely a nuisance.

A new day had come, and I eagerly anticipated a day full of sunshine. However, it was greeted with an unexpected phone call, from a group of people I desperately needed to sever ties from. God was specifically calling me out of these relationships because of their personal connections with others. Their friends were involved with dark activities and were consequently effecting my healing and spiritual growth. Although I cared deeply for them, God desired safety for me. It was a denial of truth on their behalf that back- lashed on me.

It was a memorable day. I recognized a powerful strength I possessed from the evil and anger that consumed me from these relationships. A past of dark rituals targeted my life and theirs. God was clearly showing me not only to sever these relationships, but exactly why my life depended on it.

After the provoking phone call, the next few moments became a whirlwind of evil power. It was not a power of my own, but an overpowering strength resurrected from my previous pain.

I picked up a two inch in diameter solid iron rebar that was lying on the ground. I stormed outside with a mission to release all the pain that was held inside me. I glanced at an old, abandoned, lifeless, tree stump about three feet from me. I lifted my hands above my head. Gripping this solid metal bar, I swung my arms downward, forcing a powerful strike, three times against this solid stump. My vision was clouded by my tears. I felt thirsty for retribution. Without knowing the details of my pain, I felt this deep ache burden my heart. My heart felt the injustice of life-long ritual abuse. I felt as if I was a sacrifice for too many people. I stood in silence, still clenching the bar in my hands. I was trying to calm myself down, when I felt a trickling sensation stream down my hands. I looked and saw blood running down my fingers. I realized in my rage of revenge, I had gripped the solid rebar so tightly and pounded the wood so hard that my hands were gashed open and bleeding. Without any recognition of pain, I dropped the iron rebar and went inside to clean the blood off my hands. The violence overcame me. I emerged with the memory that seemed to become even clearer to me. I did not realize the pain I caused myself. I bandaged my wounds and attempted to collect my thoughts. The anger subsided and I began to feel more like myself. It was becoming obvious that the spirit of darkness was being exposed. The memories of evil, anger, injustice, and pain were surmounting claims of desperate help.

That evening I was alone. I missed my roommates. I was worn out from the spiritual battles of the last two days. I sighed in relief as I crawled into bed. I prayed, covered my room anointing with oil, listened to worship music and read scripture. I was covered. Despite my awful day, I felt at peace going to sleep. Often, it was not a problem falling asleep, but finding myself awake in the middle of the night. It was the middle of the night I woke with a racing heart grasping to the sides of my bed. It felt as if someone was spinning my bed. It rocked side to side and then turned from front to back. I was clinging on as if I was falling off a carnival ride. I was nauseous, dizzy and frightened. My hands were clawing the side of my bed as if my life depended on it. What was happening? It was dark, and I was confused. I must be having a nightmare, I thought. I went to get out of bed, and was physically unable to stand up because the bed seemed to be spinning. My eyes were wide open, yet I could not focus on the ceiling above me. I leaped off my bed trying to adjust my vision, when I tumbled to the floor. Desperately praying for this to end, the spinning slowly stopped. I lied on the floor weeping for relief and praying- God rescue me! I cried out, "Help me Lord, I cannot do this." I feel like I am being haunted and tormented. I feel like I can't escape my own skin and the thoughts that scream at me. I am in a spiritual battle that is slowly taking my life. I constantly feel pain, fear and rage. I don't think I can survive another day of this torment. It wasn't just the external battle. I was frightened at the thought of not even being able to control the inward rage. I could feel spiritual oppression weighing on me. I felt the only way to escape this torment was death. I felt completely overwhelmed. I was tired and scared. My thoughts began to lead me down a rocky path. I found myself submitting to lies and darkness. I began to believe the lies. My head was telling me that the only way out of this oppression was to take my own life. At least then I would be at peace. I could not see the light, nor could I see any other alternatives for my life. The lies covered over my mind, and my only escape from this immense pain seemed to be death.

I had to try to dismantle the lies and dwell on positive truth. *Finally, brothers, whatever is true, whatever is noble, whatever is right, whatever is pure, whatever is lovely, whatever is admirable-if anything is excellent or praiseworthy-think about such things. (Philippians 4:8)*

I had to change my mind set. I had to suppress the emotions and mentally dwell on God's protection, and power in my life. He is worthy of praise. If I could hang on just for today, I will drive down to my friend's house. There, I will find answers in God.

I needed God's strength. It had been several days, and my head felt like it was being squeezed in a vice. It was not uncommon for me to have chronic headaches during my healing, but this time the sickening migraines increased. My body ached with pain, my joints felt as though I had been beaten. My wrists felt crushed and bound by shackles. My throat felt restricted like a noose taking my breath. My heart physically felt like someone was piercing it. My hands trembled and my spirit felt defeated by an overwhelming and relentless power. I had no desire to go on. The only thing that seemed to fill my days was fear and hatred. I felt a blood thirsty vengeance that I wasn't sure I could control anymore.

It seemed as though I was hanging from a thread, dangling over a pit of despair that I could no longer fight myself. I was just short of cutting that thin piece of thread to release my life into the grips of death. I knew in my heart that going through this healing process was tough, and it took determination and dedication to see it through. I knew God was worth it and He was able to deliver me. I knew it was the power of prayer that was keeping me alive. I couldn't entertain the thoughts of death anymore. I needed Christ to set me free, but this time the ritual acts and the exposure of these memories seemed wickedly relentless for me to give up. Despite the spiritual harassment and the physical pain of events, I needed truth.

The time was finally here. I began my commute down for my counseling session. I usually left my job and traveled down on a Tuesday. My session was not until the next day. We always enjoyed a night to catch up with each other. Most of the time, the conversation was about the week between our sessions. We would often discuss behavior modification, strategy in counseling, and occasionally something fun. Every time I made the commute it became a tradition for some of my friends to pray for me as I traveled down to her house. There was never a dull moment when I commuted. On a weekly basis, I would traverse an hour or so south to arrive at a pleasant, quiet and safe house. I was thankful for my friend's desire to see me through the roughest times of my life. I felt the Lord's peace lead me through this healing journey. However, often while I traveled from my home to her home, it would be full of exciting moments. The commute seemed challenging in and of itself. That was the first step of counseling. I encountered semi-truck trailers blowing a tire in front of me. I had a couch cushion fly off the vehicle in front of me. I was trapped for five hours in a blizzard. I witnessed a hit and run car accident. I barely escaped an oncoming car spinning out of control. This is only a few of the thrilling moments while commuting down for counseling. My travels were constantly filled with thrills and kept many of my friends on their knees praying. The commute was never boring, and I was constantly dependent on the Lord's grace to get me there safely. I wondered if the angels were on high alert when I sat in my car.

I knew with the challenges of the week, I would certainly need God's protection as I traveled down to my friend's house. I prayed to be hidden in His incomparable light. I prayed His angels would surround my vehicle on every corner. I prayed that there would be no slow traffic in the fast lane. After all, what were people thinking? Then I repented for all those times I got angry about those driving slowly in the fast lane. Regardless of my mental condition, I knew God was good to protect me as I traveled.

About a third of the way down, the acceleration of my car became dangerously in operant. It seemed unusual for me to have the pedal to the floor and not gain speed. I was not surprised when my engine light appeared on the dash near the speedometer. I was not driving an old car. This car is known for the dependability and longevity. What was happening? Even though I am a girl, I did realize this matter could not be ignored. I pushed my hazard lights on and began to guide my car to the side of the highway. This particular stretch of highway is a very busy and a popular commute. I knew I needed to exit soon. By this time my fastest speed topped at 20 mph, Semi-trucks whipped by me at 75 mph. Every time one passed me, my car swayed and surely gained an extra 5 feet or more from their momentum. I finally was able to exit and call for help. When the assistance came, it was determined that my transmission had failed. I hung my head, and refrained from crying. I hopped in the tow truck and made my way down to the mechanic. Indeed the car dealership confirmed the damage and offered me a rental car until my car was restored. Nearly five hours later I walked into my friend's house and slumped onto her couch. With my face buried in the palm of my hands, all I could do was cry. It was a week that I would never forget.

A stiff drink would guarantee a night of rest. I resigned into the extra bedroom of my friend's house. This room took on an appearance of my second home, and it felt like home. My head hit the pillow, and my body found some quality rest.

I awoke, both anticipating and dreading this new day. My friend was already downstairs preparing to work. My morning consisted of a large bowl of cereal and a mental preparation for our session. We transitioned to her living room, ready to begin discussing some of the strong triggers, emotions and fears. It was evident that reality was about to be exposed.

We began with opening up in prayer. We asked God to cover the house and property, all of our loved ones and belongings, our finances, careers and relationships with the Blood of the True Lord Jesus. We asked for divine wisdom and insight seeking His heart and His truth. We continued praying for the Lord to expose darkness, lead us in His truth, light and power. We cancelled all the wicked plans of the enemy and silenced the voice of the enemy. I prayed and said to the lord, "Whatever you want to do in my life, I give you permission. I surrender my all to you and pray for healing and freedom in my life. I rebuke any false gods or any false ideas and invite the power of the Holy Spirit to come and move in a mighty way. Lord, the one true Living God, I need a miracle and by faith I receive all that you desire to do in my life today." We continued praying and counseling, talking through memories, removing lies, receiving truth and following Christ every step. We spent time asking for deliverance from the oppression pushing me down. I was nearly two hours into prayer, and already feeling weary and tired. I wanted to rest, when an intense heat sensation came over my body. I began to remember a specific memory, and the anger that seemed to be suppressed by my weariness began to raise its ugly head. Within a brief moment of time, what I knew of myself began to drastically change again. The reality of something in my past consumed my present day body. The pain of past violence seemed to rush through my body. What was once past became very present. With great wisdom and quick reaction, my friend who had seen this before, acknowledged the situation as she began to counsel me. My tongue felt like it was on fire, almost literally. My body temperature seemed to rise, and it felt like I was captive to a superior evil presence. My body was telling me of a memory trapped inside. It was congruent to the picture unfolding in my mind. I was unsure of the physical sensations, but as the memory surfaced it was obviously confirming messages my body remembered.

I recalled aspects of the ritual act. I began to articulate what was going on. I saw dark figures that represented people, not too clearly, but obviously real. The ritual was at night in a vacant field, hidden behind structures, shrubs and a desolate space. I knew this was a familiar place, but I did not understand why I had been there. The visual memory began with what appeared to be a ritual act of witchcraft. The memory felt blurry, yet I could understand the oppressive nature of the memory. The ritual involved people summoning demons. I could taste blood in my mouth and smell a wretched aroma, yet nothing in the present day would attribute to these horrid sensations. My heart pounded, sensing severe threats, anxiety and bondage. As the memory became a little clearer, I felt danger breathing down my neck. I remembered placing my life as a sacrifice instead of another person's life. I strongly sensed the threat was to either inflict pain and torture to a friend's life, or I could take the punishment myself.

The counseling itself was in a quiet sanctuary of a living room. In the present moment, I had no reason to feel these emotions, nor sense the smell of death. These memories evolved shortly after surrendering my will to the Lord. I gave Him permission to work in my life, so I could walk in freedom. There was no implanting of suggestions, questionable guided imagery, or forced participation. It was bringing forth what I believe the Lord wanted to expose in my heart. He desired to set me free from the confines of my past. This experience was manifesting from a suppressed past, to a real present day awareness. Although this experience was powerful, I knew that God was bigger. I knew He was capable of delivering me. I knew that this experience would empower me to walk in authority and dominion over my enemy and those tormenting me. *I have given you authority to trample on snakes and scorpions and to overcome all the power of the enemy; nothing will harm you. The evil oppression was not going to linger for long. It was being exposed. (Luke 10:19)*

It wasn't the previous exposure that was convincing of this memory. It wasn't the preceding week of hell that confirmed this memory. It wasn't my background in psychology that credited the memory as a reality. It was not the obvious abuse growing up, that signaled this memory. It wasn't any one of these that convinced me that evil is real. It was building a trusting relationship with Christ, and learning to follow and discern His leading. It was an accumulation of times seeking truth and setting consecrated times to know His heart. It was moments of growth knowing that regardless of what comes my way, I will trust and believe in Him. Despite my circumstances I will follow Him. When it came to a place of not wanting to believe the horrific circumstances facing me, I still aligned my heart with the heart of Christ. I did not have to be afraid, because He would help me. The memories that were held in my mind and body only brought confirmation to the truth He was purposefully exposing.

As usual, we never forged ahead or strayed to the side of where and how God was leading. I never felt that counseling, prayer, or time following the Lord was forced. I always anticipated the Lord's presence. He desires to set the captives free. (Jesus applying this passage to Himself) *The Spirit of the Sovereign Lord is on me, because the Lord has anointed me to preach good news to the poor. He has sent me to bind up the broken hearted, to proclaim freedom for the captives and release from darkness for the prisoners, vs 2 to proclaim the year of the Lord's favor and the day of vengeance of our God, who comfort all who mourn, (Isaiah 61:1)* We pressed on for hours at a time, with occasional breaks. As the memories transpired it would co-inside with physical pain. It seemed when an aspect of the memory was released, the physical pain would be removed. I never felt like I was making this up. I felt like I finally had words that corresponded with the unexplainable pain. My heart was captive to the lies and agreements I made with darkness. It was necessary to break every covenant and vow I made while surviving ritual abuse. Often the vows were only to appear to save my life momentarily. However, I learned that vows, both good and bad are binding, and should be taken seriously. Of course, the vows and agreements to lies and darkness should be severed by the power of Jesus Christ. I often found immediate relief in repentance, forgiveness, and severing my life with the agreement of darkness.

I discovered that a sacrificial vow held me in bondage to the present pain. Growing up, I had learned the job of a "sacrifice". I played the role to sacrifice my desires, for my dad's desires. I sacrificed my life for another life. It was either the other person would be physically and mentally tortured or it would be my body that would pay the price. I had to make choices of my dog's life or my life. I constantly had to make decisions that involved extreme measures of my life or perhaps persecution for others. It seemed an obvious choice that marked me. My life was meant to be the sacrifice. My life purpose was to be the sacrifice. It was not heroic. It was a forced punishment. I felt my life purpose was to be a sacrifice. When the threats of weapons, torture and death loomed over me, it was my only choice to make harsh vows. It was all I knew.

This vow paid quite the consequences. I never intended to play God, but when I decided to vow one life for another it positioned me in a horrific spiritual warfare. Unmatched to anything I had experienced to this point, in my healing journey.

CHAPTER 11

BRIGHT MORNING STAR

It was mid-day by now, and I was already exhausted. My eyes were closed, as we were seeking the Lord. A vision appeared to me that was the most definitive visions I had experienced in my healing journey. Instantly, fear swept over my body. I heard a desperate scream off in the distance. My spirit seemed to shrink into the background. I opened my eyes to check my surroundings. I had a peculiar frown on my face. My friend asked if everything was okay. I glared at her and remained quiet as I shut my eyes again. Evil seemed to be all around me. I felt rage, murder, death and suicide were like the air I breathed. My friend remained quiet, but heard her muttering prayer. She sat witnessing me twisting and turning. I was in a spiritual battle that wanted to claim my life. I was balled into a fetal position with pain. My soul seemed entrapped in the graveyard of Hell. I was physically experiencing an undeniable fight. I felt that if this got out of control, I could hurt my friend and myself. My eyes were tightly shut and it seemed that my reality was caught in a horrific nightmare. I could cut lose. It felt as if I was physically positioned in Hell. I smelled burning sulfur. It was sickening and horrifying. The emotion of hatred felt like it was a person overpowering my own will. I suddenly hated God with everything that remained in me. My eyes burned. It was like a cutting sword came out from my eyes, desiring to destroy something. My stomach was cramped with intense pain. This seemed like a very real experience. Was I really in hell? It was a vision that seemed to be an overwhelming reality. I heard more screams. They were not words, yet I seemed to understand the underlying meaning of the scream. It was an unquenchable cry, which was only heard by the echoing of its own sound. The dark, hopeless residence of hell only seemed to remain silent over the lost souls. There were screams of desperation. There was a cry for change, yet hopeless to find it was impossible. Screams resembled a terrifying reality of eternity. I heard the crushing of what seemed like human bones. I was sickened, weakened, helpless and trapped. My eyes could only see darkness from as far to my left to my furthest point on my right. I shivered with fear and panic. Everything in this place was beyond comprehension. I did not want to be held in this captivity that was obviously, hell. I was torn between the powers of hell that held my past and a desperate cry for an escape. How could anyone believe hell is a figment of one's imagination? I heard the cries of souls that maybe once believed hell wasn't real too. I saw these beasts towering over 10' feet tall. They paced anxiously outside the prison walls of my tomb. They were horrid wretched creatures. Difficult to describe, some were massive in girth, others had wings, some sharp and distinct fangs. All were black mysterious, deceiving creatures that encircled my prison chamber. Their odor was unbearable and the surroundings insufferable. All were frightening and each had appointed assignments of deception, division and destruction. My stomach was still sick and my spirit was anxious to be released from this dark, chilling dungeon. It was painful, sickening overpowering and hopeless. It was filled with wretched smells, consuming hatred, overpowering fear and no way out. How could I find myself here? All I knew, I had some hope in me, that God could get me out of here. It was not too late for me. I knew this was not my eternal destination at this point in my life. Perhaps, Christ was showing me, without Him saving me several times from ritual acts, this could have been my eternal home.

Although this was very real, I was grateful this was a vision. I opened my eyes to a very bright assurance. My body was clenched and paralyzed by the shocking glimpse of hell. Despite the presence of strong and evil emotions, I knew my first step was to repent for all the vows of being a willing sacrifice to evil. I had made a commitment to vow to evil and rebel against God exchanging life for life. I was not meant to be a god over my life. Only Jesus was meant to be the ultimate sacrifice for all mankind. *He is the atoning sacrifice for our sins, and not only for ours but also for the sins of the whole world. (1 John 2:2)* Jesus is the Lord over my life. I quickly repented and asked the Lord for forgiveness for every vow and act I committed against Him and others. When we repent it releases the ground of the enemy over that area in our hearts. When we repent, and align our hearts with the Lord, He will faithfully deliver us.

After a sincere repentance and a strong desire to embark upon a strategy to eradicate my week of living hell, I sought the Lord for His divine intervention. I knew I could not do this on my own. I could not rescue myself from a pit of hell. I could not muster enough strength to help myself. I was really at the bottom of my life. It would only be Christ that could rescue me from hell. All I could do was accept my powerlessness, submit, recognize and accept the grace of God, and by faith ask Him to rescue me from bondage of hell. My vows had made this vision of hell, real. My participation in evil would have sent me to hell. It was my bondage of pain, lies and belief system trapped me in a life simulating hell. My heart was burdened with death, hopelessness and fear. It was time for God to set every area free.

I was standing on God's promise of His desire to free me. This time, as I closed my eyes, the vision closed in on me, but my body was less tense. I stood silently, in this cold, dark, brick layered dungeon. I couldn't view much out of my iron barred window. I could only hear the piercing shrieks in the distance. Everything was the same, but this time I held onto hope. I stood on my tip toes, peering out the small prison window and caught a glimpse of the destructive beasts that patrolled between me and a rod iron black gate. I don't know what the gate represented. I only sensed it was like an entrance gate. It towered a couple of stories tall, and was guarded by these ghastly beasts. There was a vast endless expanse of darkness beyond the gate. Although I knew hope was around the corner, it was still a terrifying place to be in. I was chilled to the bone and I was panting in silence.

I trembled in the daunting, dark chamber. I waited for my redeemer to rescue me. My hands were tightly wrapped around the prison bars. I repented, forgave and silenced the voice and power of the enemy by the blood and power of Christ. The room I was presently sitting in, was quiet and still. My spirit lifted within me. The picture I began to see was very clear. Although my eyes were closed, it seemed like the eyes of my spirit were wide-open. I was captivated by a small light in the distance. I peered into the distance, and caught a glance of a small but distinct, bright light. I took a deep breath, knowing it wasn't there a few minutes ago. This unique and intriguing circle of light appeared in the void of the darkness. It caught my eye and continued to hold my attention. My eyes drew intently towards this light, when I heard a faint voice whispering to my spirit, "I am the bright morning star". Hope surged my heart. I began to anticipate a closer encounter with this light. As this presence of light grew brighter and closer, I began to notice the strong emotions and physical pain began to dissipate. The fear, anger and all the pain I held quickly relinquished. I perched myself up on my tip toes, clutching the black iron bars so that I could see this light transform before me. Before I was able to calculate the time, the light enlarged from a small circle to a blinding spotlight. I was only able to see a silhouette of a magnificent horse and a rider. As His presence emerged from the light, it was a sensation more powerful than words. I stood in awe, admiring this massive horse and the apparent rider who had a mission to rescue me. I began to loosen my grip on the bars and became completely enthralled with the power and passion that had driven this rider and His horse to such a place to rescue me. The horse stopped outside my prison walls. Although he towered over me and the light nearly blinded me, the presence of the horse and rider was overwhelming. I am sure it was only a brief moment, but I could sense this strong pursuit and mighty purpose from this heavenly horse. I stared at this magnificent creature. I realized in my heart, this horse had depth and passion in his eyes. It seemed like he knew why he was there. I was the reason. He confidently carried the purpose of the one who rode upon him. Even though I was intrigued by this horse, it did not completely distract me from the rider, who had descended from the horse. I felt weak in my entire body and exhausted in my spirit, yet the strength of His presence empowered me to press on. I knew this was a divine experience. I turned my eyes away from the beauty and presence of this magnificent horse, seeking the Almighty Deliverer. The mysterious rider already passed by me. This all happened so rapidly that I can't even calculate an approximate time. It was after turning my attention from the horse to my savior, that I recognized two profiles in the corner of my occupied dungeon. One stood hunched over, crippled and powerless, hidden in the dark. He was allusive, cowardly and couldn't handle the light. He wasn't able to lift his head or eyes to the Almighty who stood in power and light. I could faintly hear their short conversation. It was simple, yet a powerful claim. The rider was Jesus Christ. He stood between me and the dark, shriveled accuser. My spirit was attentive to the brief interaction. In all clarity and authority, I heard the voice of Jesus speak on my behalf. His voice shook the walls of my prison. The darkness fled. My spirit connected to the triumphant declaration over me. Jesus said, "This One Is Mine". I fully received His truth in my heart and celebrated His power to deliver me. In an instant my spirit was removed from darkness to light. My heavy burden and despair was diminished and the truth of the true Lord Jesus set me free.

CHAPTER 12

TO HIM WHO OVERCOMES

In a flash, the experience of hell was transformed into an experience in heaven. My spirit was caught up in a vision that radiated an array of beauty, and flooded my spirit with unsurpassable feelings of wholeness and life. I never looked back. I did not question the transformation; I just continued to walk in a place that I knew was heaven. The breathtaking landscape was vast and brilliant. I stood in awe of the most magnificent scenery. The snow capped peaks of the mountains reached the blue canopy above. The colors bounced off the mountains with deep luminosity. Every color was glowing with life. The sky was a perfect shade of blue. The rushing water fell over the steep rocky cliffs with a source of power and tranquility. The greens were vibrant and full of life. My eyes observed new brilliance of colors and landscape. Nothing on earth could compare to this canvas of creation. My nose was awakened with senses of beauty and fragrance combined with an inner aroma of serenity. The valley was vast, embracing gardens of wild flowers. The warmth of light brought a peace and safety I had never experienced in my life. My spirit began to experience life in a new and powerful way. It is difficult to describe what my eyes saw, but even more difficult to depict the experience my spirit embraced. I was in a place full of life. The old was gone and the power of "new" entered into my heart. *Therefore, if anyone is in Christ, he is a new creation; the old has gone and the new has come! (2 Corinthians 5:17)* There was no fear, doubt, anger, anymore. I was filled with joy, peace and life. Every oppressive spirit was completely gone, and my heart encountered light permeating to my core. I was free. I could feel it spiritually and physically. I never imagined Heaven to be so exquisite.

The Presence of God

I realized I was not alone. The greatest miracle of this transformation was standing beside my Savior. I was humbled in His presence. He was my hero. Who else could have saved me? He had mercy upon me. He forgave me. He delivered me. This was not a figment of my imagination. This was real and He did not fail me in my darkest hour. He was the only one who had the power to enter my hell, rescue me and bring me into an eternal hope. His eyes were full of deep compassion and love. His voice melted and washed away the strongholds of my heart and mind. He whispered so gently, yet so powerfully. His truth weaved to the depths of my heart releasing the restrictions of my past. His voice thundered, diminishing my enemy to a voiceless, powerless, withered coward. Jesus removed my chains and opened doors for His life and healing to flood my entire body, spirit and mind. By his power, I was removed from the pit of hell and uplifted.

With the presence of the Lord around me, new beginnings seem to dawn on the horizon. I admired the astonishing vibrant picture of heaven. I turned my head slowly side to side, embracing all that was near and far from me. In the distance, I caught glimpse of a circling eagle. My mind recognized something different about this creature. He ascended to great heights over the mountain tops and began to loop back towards me. He soared effortlessly in my direction. I watched intently and anticipated a closer look. My senses were on high alert. I began to tune my ears towards the remarkable sound it was making. As this magnificent eagle approached, my focus was concentrated on His extraordinary communication. The squalling seemed to have purpose and meaning, yet I could not understand. His quickening approach enthralled me. This was no ordinary eagle. This large eagle was much greater than any eagle I knew on earth. This creature circled above me, and appeared to be human size with amazing wings. I stood in silence, fully targeting this eagle. The sound of the eagle was intriguing. I tried to silence my thoughts and concentrate on the noise it was making. I simply did not understand. Then quietly with a gentle whisper, I heard the Lord speak to my heart. He said, "I want to open your ears to sounds of the spirit". Simultaneously, I began to hear the resounding joyful praises the eagle was declaring. The eagle glided above giving honor and praise to the King. I closed my eyes and allowed the ears of my spirit to join in with the praises to our King. The eagle rejoiced singing, "Holy, Holy is the Lord God almighty, who was and is and is to come." And once again, Holy, Holy is the Lord God almighty, who was and is and is to come. My spirit promptly joined in one accord with a heart of worship and celebration. I opened my eyes again and witnessed the Lord extending His right arm, slowly moving left to right, displaying a perfect splendor before my eyes. He began to speak to me, "You are in my throne room." *The first living creature was like a lion, the second was like an ox, the third had a face like a man, the fourth was like a flying eagle. Vs 8 Each of the four living creatures had six wings and was covered with eyes all around even under the wings. Day and night they never stop saying "Holy, holy, holy is the Lord God Almighty, who was and is, and is to come."* (*Revelations 4: 7*) My knees weakened, my heart skipped a beat. I was honored, humbled and filled with gratitude. I was astonished at the divine exchange occurring and unfolding in my life. I was experiencing a true, brilliant and spectacular reality of Heaven. *To him who overcomes, I will give the right to sit with me on my throne, just as I overcame and sat down with my Father on His throne. (Revelations 3:21)*

I love being in the presence of the Lord. I didn't want to leave. I wanted to explore and learn. The Lord delighted in my time with Him and wanted to show me many things. I desired to be a good student. Since He is my creator, He knew my interests. He knew the way I would learn. He knew what would make me grow. He knew what would make me want more of Him. I had a great opportunity to learn about Him. The Bible and character of Jesus was alive in a new way that I could understand. As I waited and listened in His presence, He began to speak more to me. He was watching me gaze at the eagle. His affection rested on me, as my face illuminated with joy. My heart was filled and quenched with pleasure. I did not long for anything, but to be in His presence, and admire my surroundings. He delighted in my thankful heart. He was overjoyed and singing over me. *Sing, O Daughter of Zion; shout aloud, O Israel! Be glad and rejoice with all your heart, O Daughter of Jerusalem! The Lord has taken away your punishment, He has turned back your enemy. The Lord, the King of Israel, is with you; never again will you fear any harm. On that day they will say to Jerusalem, Do not fear, O Zion; do not let your hands hang limp. The Lord your God is with you, He is mighty to save. He will take great delight in you, He will quiet you with His love, He will rejoice over you with singing. (Zephaniah 3:14-17)*

He showed me He wanted to increase my vision and hearing. He desired to give me good gifts. He wanted to increase my faith through discernment, wisdom, spiritual ears and eyes. I was amazed in all I went through; He wanted to give me more. He wanted me to soar like the eagle with new perspective, with a broader and more precise vision. He wanted to increase good things in my life. This was His desire. Not once did my power accomplish anything. It was His power through faith that set my feet on solid, holy ground. The demonstration of His love elevated to great heights.

The Lord graciously and sincerely welcomed me with passion and love into His throne room. However, He wanted me to follow Him to the next adventure. As I adjusted my eyes from the endless skies and the enthralling eagle, to the footsteps of my path, I realized I was well above the seascape. Being that I am not too fond of heights, I slowly stepped back in caution leaning my back against a rocky cliff. The all knowing Jesus understood my thoughts of concern. Without saying a word, the Lord knew I was suddenly aware of the heights I was standing on. I was not fearful, but in my trance of amazement with the eagle, I simply did not know the heights in which my feet were standing upon. I wondered, how did I get up here? The Lord initiated a soft whisper in response to my thoughts. He said, "It has been all the tough times, the obstacles, heartaches, the times of testing, the never giving up, the pain and tears, and the triumphs that elevated you to this level of faith in your life." As I glanced below, I saw a steep drop off, with sides of flat iron rock. I said, "But I don't understand." The Lord kindly replied, "All those trials strengthened your faith to new heights and knowledge of Me." It began to make sense. All those times when I prayed increased my faith. Those times I endured pain stepped me closer to dependence with the Lord. Several times when I wanted to give up, He helped me place one foot in front of the other. He empowered me to press on, and seek Him. Those struggle were the times when the Lord was refining my faith through perseverance. The countless times of tears, and heart-ache, were the moments that faith brought me to the heart of Christ. When I could not see, faith prevailed. Sometimes, when I think God is not moving fast enough; I needed to realize that His work was perfectly orchestrated for the power of His glory to be revealed. Although I was terrified, He was not. He knew from start to finish the perfection of His healing in my life. My healing was complete in Him; I just needed to journey through every key in His timing.

Is any one of you in trouble? He should pray. Is anyone happy? Let him sing songs of praise. Is any one of you sick? He should call the elders of the church to pray over him and anoint him with oil in the name of the Lord. And the prayer offered in faith will make the sick person well; the Lord will raise him up. If he has sinned he will be forgiven. Therefore confess your sins to each other and pray for each other so that you may be healed. The prayer of a righteous man is powerful and effective. (James 5:13-16)

Now standing near the top of mountain towering over the greenery of the valley, I realized my relationship with the Lord was stronger than I imagined. He was showing me a place of intimacy that I developed through my trials. All those times when I felt weak, Christ allowed those times to make me strong. All the while I felt I was in a pit of failure, defeat and endless misery, He was elevating me closer to Him through faith. He was raising me up to see a far greater purpose than the valley below. I experienced a different view with greater consequences if I fell, and it seemed to require more of me. He continued to speak to me, "Not many get to experience these great heights and levels, and some remain on the valley floor and explore the fruit and trees and water provided. Yet others will climb to rocky levels and give up. Still others will scale to plateaus and be content. Few will ascend to great heights to see the rewards of faith in their lives." Though I knew not to judge the others for the level of faith where they remained, I wanted to encourage many to press on in order to experience life with much greater views, a greater perspective, balance, experience, faith and intimacy with Christ. To stand above the hardships of my life and experience closeness with Him was worth it all.

I was able to receive this gift of intimacy through my struggle of hardships. Sharing in His sufferings comes with at a costly sacrifice.

God gave His only son. His plan of redemption was at an enormous cost. Therefore, when I entered into this healing journey, I enrolled in a practical, "hands on" school of faith. It is the process struggle when my strength was relinquished, that I experienced the mighty power of God. He is worth the pain, in order to gain life in Him.

The Lord constantly kept me from falling. It was never in my power, strength or might. This healing journey was the most difficult climb of my life. Every week we were experiencing miracle after miracle. This vision of Christ elevating me to heights in the heavenly realm was a true experience. It took a team effort and relentless perseverance it took to get to this place of freedom.

In awe of this insightful truth, I stood in silence taking it all in. The Lord waited until I directed my eyes back to Him. He said, "Let's continue." We sauntered along a narrow pathway not much wider than two people in width. It was a rocky trail winding around the mountainside. Even though I towered over the meadowland, I still had not reached the summit. I followed Christ's leading before me.

We came to a stopping point. He directed His face toward the mountainside and His back faced the valley. He raised His head upward elevating His chin. He looked up toward the top of the mountain, then back to me. He smiled. My eyes widened in curiosity of what He was implying. I convincingly told him, "I can't climb that". He kindly reminded me, I had already climbed to this height. He said, "Let's try". We faced a vertical, flat and smooth edge rock. I looked at it and frowned. My mind questioned my ability. My heart assured me. It was not about my ability, it was the degree of faith. I reached my hand up on the flat iron rock searching for a good hand hold. I would not let the giant before me defeat me. I needed to trust Jesus standing before me. I will follow Him. After all, I have gone this far and He proved to be trustworthy, I need to trust Him as we embark upon another adventure. I looked at Him and His eyes displayed a pleasure and reassurance. He held a strong confidence in our relationship. He trusted me to try. I trusted Him not to fail. I could not see, but faith required me to believe. Without delay, I reached up and grabbed an edge. The rock was long and strong enough to get a solid hold. I began to pull up with my right hand, while my left hand and feet were searching frantically for another hand and foot hold. Simultaneously, as I believed enough to reach for the rock, the formations of rock became visually apparent. I began to scale this dangerous rock ledge in a fluent matter. I realized, the climb was becoming effortless. Within a brief amount of time I grasped this concept of faith even more. Climbing alongside me was Jesus. He wanted me to know He was right there by my side. I guess I viewed the "walk of faith" as an individual sport. I realized, He empowered me to believe. Because His faith was in me, I had the faith required to do the work. I did not let doubt over- rule my desire to please Him. He released the exact measure of solid ground, in order for me to grasp what I needed to climb higher. Faith was a team effort of His character, power and my willingness.

I reached the peaking point, for the moment. Although I was not out of breath, I wanted to soak in another breath-taking view of endless beauty. I viewed encompassing streams of life, mountains of faith, meadows of peace and the inviting beauty of spectacular color and warmth. I rested, revisiting the detail of the climb and interested to understand more the journey of faith.

It seemed like as I followed Him, and enjoyed His presence, my heart desired to be filled with more of Him. I learned that ultimate faith was walking in the ultimate recognition and knowledge of the Father. By faith I am alive. Through faith I experienced a new life full of His love. Through faith in Jesus I entered a life beyond my own efforts, and above anything of my own accomplishments.

I began to understand that faith pleases God. As I stood watching the eagle circle around me and began to listen and understand new things in faith, God was receiving and delighting in my faith. While my head was tilted towards the eagle, I was eagerly listening to the praises released. In faith, I joined in praise, and the Lord inhabited my praise with great delight.

Additionally, faith and humility go hand in hand. Honest humility is agreeing with truth. In humility, I prayed and submitted to Christ. When I prayed, faith rose within my heart. Christ empowered my faith to envision Him in His glory. In His presence I was able to glean wisdom. *When pride comes, then comes disgrace, but with humility comes wisdom. (Proverbs 11:2)*

Finally, walking in faith never left me complacent. As long as I was willing, faith in Christ surpassed my personal limitations. Through faith I was able to experience the power of God. God demonstrates His power that we may know His love.

Now faith is being sure of what we hope for and certain of what we do not see. (Hebrews 11:1)

CHAPTER 13

THE SOURCE OF LIGHT

I began to realize over time, the powerful transformation taking place in my life. The agonizing work was liberating my mind. I was seeing myself in a new light. My mind was not controlled by threats and evil. I would offer grace, instead of skepticism. I believed in the power of light and truth, over darkness and lies. The journey was long, with an extensive amount of work that still needed to be done, but I could see gradual changes in my heart. I was getting stronger. I realized during my intense healing moments, I felt surrounded by darkness. I know the Lord was exposing the darkness so that He could remove it. However, I did not realize how much the darkness affected me, until I began to see the power of His light in my life. His light severed the power of darkness from my past, and He placed me in His light holding my present and future. *My God turns my darkness into light. (Psalm 18:28)*

I prayed that His light would shine upon me. I wanted to live in light. I wanted to understand His light. A powerful portrait displayed before me. I was spending time in the Lord's presence. He began to open up an astounding revelation of His light. I was quietly seeking the Lord in worship. I began to pray, inviting His presence to show me something new about the Lord. I desired for my heart to connect with His. I longed for ways to know Jesus better. I sat in the peace of my living room, when the Lord expanded insight of His light. This picture captivated my spirit.

My eyes were closed. A warm sensation blanketed my body. I anticipated a divine moment in His presence. In this vision I was standing. I began to look around. I love God's creation and enjoy observing the magnificent beauty of His hands. As I turned around, I noticed an array of colors. I was fascinated by the beaming lights dancing in an orderly fashion. I stood admiring the various shades of rainbow colors. Not one shade seemed to be left out. It felt like each color listened to the director so delicately. He was orchestrating this symphony of beauty. As I looked a little closer to the colors and the origin of this masterful show of lights, I began to see the colors dance from the presence of Christ. The lights came directly from Him, rising from the middle of His spirit beaming upward and outward, swirling in various directions with meaning and purpose. I was baffled and in awe of this orchestration. The light listened to His movement. He never spoke. The light streamed from Him. It was radiating and originating from Him. The magnificent colors of green, yellow, blue, orange, purple and red were flowing from Him. His hands moved and the colors bounced twirling around Him. Joy filled me. I was recognizing His awesome creation of light. He did not just create light. He is the source of light. His display of spender was absolutely stunning. I witnessed a colorful current of beauty and peace, collide with power and light. I saw my creator arrange the light of life.

Outside of my counseling sessions my life and heart was constantly dependent on the Lord. I spent many hours seeking Him. Spending time with the Lord were necessary periods of my life, ordained by Him for healing and wholeness. I desired to find my life in Him. I longed to dive to the depths of His love for me. Therefore, when He revealed indescribable images of light, love, and redemption, I held onto these promises. His promises carried me through. *For you have delivered me from death and my feet from stumbling, that I may walk before God in the light of life. (Psalm 56:13)*

The Lord's light was shining on me. My eyes were open to the light of life, which was not an easy task. Much more lies ahead of me, but I can see the glory of the Lord ahead of me.

Arise, shine, for your light has come, and the glory of the Lord rises upon you. See, darkness covers the earth and thick darkness is over the peoples, but the Lord rises upon you and his glory appears over you. (Isaiah 60:1-2) My life transformed from darkness to light. It was not by my power, but it was the Light that lived in me. The darkness fled and the source of light appeared over me.

CHAPTER 14

WALKING WITH JESUS

A good portion of my time with the Lord, I felt was all "business". I benefited from His mighty work. We both collaborated to accomplish His plans for me. A wonderful friendship developed. However, a large portion of my life was stressful, traumatizing and simply not fun. I wanted to enjoy moments with the Lord, where I could sit and learn. I was not great at memorizing scripture. I struggled staying focused and my eyes jump all over the page. It would be difficult for me to concentrate. I would still read His Word, but He knew visions would grab my attention, and then I would seek His word for truth. God knows how I learn, grow and trust in Him.

I was lying in bed one afternoon resting and praying. I began to ask the Lord some general questions. I quieted my mind and caught sight of a vision. I was walking in the heavenly realm. Initially, I was alone. I faced an open terrain expanding far greater than I could see. The scenery was spectacular. I could hear this powerful rush of water nearby. I followed the thundering noise, until the most amazing waterfall appeared ahead. The waterfall was extraordinary. It was forceful in nature and magnetizing to my spirit. The water surged over the country-side as if it came from nowhere. The clear rushing water dropped over jagged wet boulders nearly fifty feet below. The waterfall was tremendous in power. I stopped gazing and decided to hike a short jaunt up and to the side of the water. I ascended slowly, as I admired the pleasant surroundings. I reached the top. Before me was a beautiful panoramic view of this gorgeous meadow. I could see mountains in the distance. My heart and eyes marveled at the soft country land, sprinkled with the fragrance of sweet delicate flowers. A stream flowed by my side. Its current was swift, supplying the power behind the waterfall. I walked alongside the stream, finding nourishment to my soul. The sound of the water was refreshing. I leaped on and off boulders while I sauntered along. The knee high grass slowly swayed with the gentle breeze. The various shades of green grass were soft to the touch of my feet. The landscape was simple and pure. It was warm and inviting, a peaceful place to rest.

I surveyed the grounds in curiosity. My eyes became acquainted with both familiar and new creatures. I wasn't frightened by the animals. I was intrigued and fascinated. Off in the distance, amidst the majestic prairie, resided an old beaten and rugged shack. It represented a once creatively designed structure. The wood was warped with rotten boards and a splintered and broken foundation. Perhaps this was once a well designed home that carried memories of laugher love and hope; but now seemed half withered and unable to hold the promises of a future. As I continued forward for a closer look, Jesus appeared before me. I was very pleased He was there with me. I knew this heavenly place was made perfect in His presence. I knew He would be able to give me insight to this puzzling vision. He looked at this shack with attentiveness and purpose. He softly glided His hand over the wood, as though His mind was transforming the decomposed wood. His face beamed with endless joy. His face expressed a wonderful sense of creativity. He spoke to me with delight bubbling in His voice. A soft tenderness arose from His voice saying, "I love broken things". This old shack seemed to be close to His heart. With sincerity and passion in His heart, I knew it wasn't that He desired the death and decay of things; it was that He sought opportunity to restore the broken and abandoned things. This house obviously represented a special place in His heart. I stood waiting for more insight. His face displayed a mindful and strategic reconstruction of this shack. His love was revealed with His every tender touch. At once, He turned to me with a soft curl in His mouth, He said, "Let's continue on." Uncertain of His plan, I knew I could trust the journey. In my heart I knew we were moving ahead, but would return to this spot with greater insight. Although the shack was quickly eroding, the ground on which this house stood was a divine foundation. I knew there was still hope for this little shack.

Jesus and I were walking side by side. He was on my right as we stepped in perfect synchronized form. I found myself looking at Him, watching His beauty flow and radiate every second. I could not verbalize His all encompassing radiance, power and tenderness. His presence and glory are too difficult for my brain to articulate. I know my spirit felt like I was one with Him. I was at home, a place where love truly made me whole. We journeyed along for a brief moment, when I recognized to my left side there was a lion. I have to admit, I take great delight in His creation of animals. I was so elated and filled with a child- like excitement. I couldn't believe I had this ferocious lion striding alongside me. It seemed like a dream come true. Without hesitation, I knew this was a gift from the Lord. I immediately grabbed the Lord's hand to hold, offering him a humble thanksgiving.

When I reached to grasp His hand, I noticed an inscription on His palm. The mark signified something deeper than just my name. His hands held my story of torture and pain. He carried the detail of my pain on His hand, yet the pain of my life was in the exact place where He was nailed to the cross. Although it was quite difficult to fully comprehend. The moment was very powerful. My pain was covered by the redemption of the cross. His scar covered over my pain. He conquered the deathly attacks against Him and my life. I was desperately attempting to grip the measure of His love. I held His hand open, resting in mine. I traced His palm. My life was detailed in the palm of His hand. I realized how intimately He carried the pain of my life. It was mind boggling to comprehend the knowledge of my life was ingrained in the palm of Jesus Christ, my Savior. They were the same hands that shed precious blood for my life. The awe of His closeness took awhile to accept. Every tear of mine that was shed, was held in His hands. The intricacy of my life was imprinted on Him. My name was held by the Creator of the universe. He knew me. My name not marked in ink. My name was marked with detail, permanent fixation on His hand. *See, I have engraved you on the palms of my hands; your walls are ever before me. (Isaiah 49:16)*

I was in awe of what I was witnessing. I knew that through all the healing, visions and countless times I depended on God a foundation of trust was established. Through the terrifying moments I learned to value God's faithfulness. The times I felt alone were often the times I felt His presence the most. Through the intricate healing journey, I realized my faith was growing stronger. My love for Christ was growing deep. When I did not understand the situation, His truth would make things clearer for me. Accusations and trials pierced me, but the Lord's presence assured me. He understood. In my darkest hours, I experienced the most triumphal relationship of my life. When I surrendered everything, He made me into more than I could have imagined. There has been nothing, in comparison to this great journey. He was taking the scattered pieces of my life, and building a heart full of love, gifts and life. The desires I had faded. But, when I grabbed hold of His desires for me; it brought new hope. All that I wanted did not matter, in comparison to knowing His love for me. I was use to being a sacrifice for evil. Evil brought death, torture, loss and extensive pain. When I surrendered my life to Christ, I gained life. I felt what it was like, to live. It was good. *For whoever wants to save his life will lose it, but whoever loses his life for me will save it. What good is it for a man to gain the whole world, and yet lose or forfeit his very self? (Luke 9:24, 25)*

I witnessed the power unfolding in this vision of His hand. Just grabbing His hand gave me insight of how much my life was truly in His hand. He empowered my faith and healing. He orchestrated every detail of my life. His love is worth it all. He carries it all.

I clasped His hand as we journeyed forward. I began to ask Him questions. At times, I felt as though I could barely understand or hear what He was speaking to me. It was then I reminded myself that my mind, logic and fleshly reasoning can get in the way of what God was trying to communicate. I needed to keep pushing back the familiar and analytical part of my mind to enjoy the presence of God and His truth.

I quieted my mind and thoughts, meditating on Jesus. The vision became clear again. Jesus was before me, to the right side. I extended my hand for His hand. It was the same hand that I was holding, before my thoughts got in the way. When my right hand reached for His left hand, I could not join them together. I tried again. I felt this gentle spirit speak to me. "I am not offering you my left hand." I asked, "Why not?" I felt the Lord say, "You are grabbing on to the old. You are reaching for the familiar. I want to lift you up and place you on My right side."

I paused for a minute. My eyes were opened before me, and I saw His mighty right hand extended toward me. In the past, He was on my right side. *I saw the Lord always before me. Because He is at my right hand, I will not be shaken. (Acts 2:25)*He did not want me to grab what was familiar of my past anymore. He wanted me to grab a hold of my future with Him. When I repositioned myself, I grabbed a hold of His right hand. I realized this was a position of honor, protection, authority, and a promising future. *The Lord say, to my Lord: sit at my right hand until I make your enemies a footstool for your feet. Psalm 118:15-16 Shouts of joy and victory resound in the tents of the righteous; The Lord's right hand has done mighty things! The Lord's right hand is lifted high; the Lord's right hand has done mighty things! (Psalm 10:1)* I did not want to live out of the familiar pain. I wanted to grab hold of His promises for my future. He was offering His plan of power, victory and mighty things. Therefore, I refused the familiar patterns and learned behaviors of my past, and stepped in faith to receive victory.

I looked at Him, with confidence and anticipation. His eyes displayed pleasure and delight. He assured me, great things were ahead. He wanted to renew my life and mind. He wanted to restore my thought patterns. He wanted to bring life into the areas of my life that held death. He desired to bring hope back to me. He wanted me to understand that He was offering His hand to say, I overcame. He has positioned me on the right side where my enemies have been defeated.

His hand softly embraced my hand. He encouraged me to step forth in faith and begin to see the display of His marvelous wonders. I began to see great, exuberant, brilliant lights dancing within my vision, but even greater within my spirit. The lights seemed to bring life, and I found myself delighting in this beauty. I turned to the Lord, and asked Him, "What are these lights?" He responded by saying, "This is the light of my resurrection power. I want you to live in my resurrection power." *I want to know Christ and the power of His resurrection and the fellowship of sharing in His sufferings, becoming like Him in His death, and so, somehow, to attain to the resurrection from the dead. (Philippians 3:10)*

He continued looking me in the eyes. He said, "Be free in the truth. I am your God and great I AM. Proclaim and decree the right side of

God from this day forth in my life. Today is a new beginning." I stood in His presence taking it all in. In my own power, I would not be able to walk this out. I prayed the power of the Holy Spirit to ignite and deepen this revelation.

Our journey was full of enlightenment and enjoyment of each other. In our path ahead, lied a pool of deep mud. It was like quick sand. The mud surely meant to be death if I stepped in it. However, because I was walking in His presence, I was able to see the trap ahead. I asked the Lord, "What is that?" He responded by saying, "It is a portion of your life that still needs work." I squinted my eyebrows together, baffled in thought. Perhaps, I misunderstood all that He just showed me. "Wait," I said. "I thought my past was gone." He said, "Yes, your enemies are defeated. Your past has been removed. The healing that continues will be different, because you live out of my power, not your own. It won't be from the life you knew. It will be from the life you now live through me. Therefore your healing will not sink you. Your thought patterns will not drown you anymore. Your beliefs will not drag you under. Instead, you will be able to overcome the obstacles ahead of you through My presence. There will be obstacles in life, but now my revelation will empower you to see differently." I guess I understood. There will always be challenges ahead. Although my healing always invited the Holy Spirit, maybe the mindset of living in His resurrection power would transform my outlook on my healing. His resurrection power would dismantle the depression, and free me to receive more of Him.

I took a deep breath in and exhaled. I was trying to receive His wisdom. Either I did not fully grasp the concept or He wanted to show me more. Out of the corner of my eyes, I noticed in one of His hands was a white blob of paint. On the other hand, there was a black blob of paint. I was puzzled, but intrigued. He clapped His hands together, rubbing them side to side. He opened the face of His hands. They were a blurry mess of gray. The colors were not distinct. Instead, the paint was a muddled mess. I wrinkled my nose in disgust. What was He showing me? His picture was clear. He began to explain a few things to me. He was using a little repetition to teach me. I cannot mix the things of the past, with the new things He has for me. It will leave me confused, lost and disappointed. The enemy wants to kill, steal and destroy. If I struggle with doubt, it will steal from my faith. If I don't walk in the faith of His resurrection power in my life, it will destroy me. If I allow the destruction of my past to win, it will kill me. Living a mixed thought life will bring death. We believe what we think. We will live out what we believe. The black matter is symbolic of my thoughts, reactions, and my belief system of my past. (Anger, fear, hatred) The white blob represents the good promises of my future. I cannot grab a hold of my future with the reactions of my past. I cannot walk out a life of light, as long as I am still in fear and disbelief. I escaped my past because God was with me. The gray matter is when I walk in rejection, failure, hopelessness, and then try in my own power to overcome. The gray matter is when I dream good things, but wallow in self pity. I must live in His life of freedom, not the bondage of my past. *Neither do men poor new wine into old wineskins. If they do, the skins will burst, the wine will run out and the wineskins will be ruined. No, they pour new wine into new wineskins, and both are preserved. (Matthew 9:17)*

He showed me, a lot of people live in gray. People walk in wounds of their past. People in ministry teach out of the gray areas in their lives. It is in those gray areas that mixture is taught. It can be those gray areas where pain is received. The gray areas are where people give up. They lose homes, marriages, hope and fall victim to the brokenness of their hearts. God has more to offer than the gray areas. The gray area represents confusion, hopelessness, defeat and discouragement. It is in the gray areas that people seek to fill voids. It is in the gray areas that people are not whole. It is a dangerous area. It is not where the whole truth resides. Don't be deceived in the gray matter of confusion. Life is in the purity, whiteness of His truth.

We continued our journey along a rather flat meadowland. The country was filled with beautiful flowers. We arrived at a tall tree. It was standing alone, distant from any other structure. I have often wondered if trees could speak, what story they would tell. This tree, if it could speak, would be a legend. It had a solid wide girth, demonstrating wisdom in age. It towered above us, full of tender green leaves providing a shaded area of rest. Near the solid tree there was a neatly anchored wood carved bench. The seat covered by the coolness of shade, but also with little glimmers of sunlight spotting the smooth surface of the bench. It was quaint, quiet and perfect.

As we took a seat, I started to chat with the Lord. He seemed very content, sitting on the bench. I watched Him for a moment. I realized I did not have to make conversation with Him. Not that I felt I needed too, I just wanted to talk to Him. But, in admiring Him, I rather enjoyed sitting, quietly in His presence. We sat together. I found the quiet time refreshing. It was fulfilling. His love was quieting me. I sensed He longed for His people to just be still and live, rest and be happy in His presence. I knew I was guilty many times for wanting to have answers. I was guilty for not being still. I was accountable many times for being "busy". At this moment, I understood the power of sitting still. As my heart gave thanks, (in a worshipful manner) all other topics that would normally cause me to wiggle; faded away.

I was fully content. When I made eye contact with the Lord, He said, "Watch this." He unfolded His right hand. In the palm of His hand, was a pile bird seed. I was amazed. In a short amount of time, a beautiful bird came and ate out of His hand. I watched intently His interaction with this tiny feathered friend. Indeed, that is just what he was, a friend of God. The bird knew he was safe in His hand. He knew the creator of his little life. I giggled out loud. It was amazing. God cared and provided for his little life. The bird did not ask, "Can I take some for tomorrow"? The amount was exactly what the little bird needed. The bird trusted in Christ. I asked Jesus, "Can I try"? He said, "Yes". I thought the Lord would pour seed into my hand. Instead, I opened my palm (to my surprise) and seed filled the creases of my hand. My hand was filled with provision for this little friend. The bird jumped from His hand to mine. I think the bird knew I was safe. I saw joy light the eyes of the Lord. An opportunity for my passion, to care for animals, brought pleasure to the Lord. He smiled, and He giggled out loud.

I felt it was okay to ask the Lord some questions. I directed my face towards God. I asked, "What is this journey about"? He said, "Restoration, resurrection, release". He desires to restore my life. He wants me to live out of His resurrection power, and release me into the passions He has given me. I began to see the evolution of the journey. I recalled the old shack. I witnessed the love in His eyes, to restore something that was broken. I remembered grabbing a hold of His hand. He wanted me to walk in His mighty works. He was teaching me to walk in alignment of His promises. He wanted me to walk in His resurrection power. Now, I was here with Him. He was unfolding provision for me to walk in my dreams. I was amazed. I still had a journey of healing ahead of me. However, He wanted to give me hope of His plans, and a prosperous future. He did not want me to remain in a life of healing. He wants to release me, into freedom of who He created me to be. The healing is not who I am. The past is not who I am. It is the journey of perseverance, determination, strength and a willing heart to seek Christ at all costs, to become the woman He created me to be. It was about a journey in His presence. It is about a life walking with Christ. The vision was a reminder that it is not about the "doing", it is about "being". While being in His presence, I was restored, preserved, and brought to life. I realized, I was missing the bigger picture sometimes, when my only focus was about me. I was learning all the time, when I was with Him. The journey taught me that the demand of all the questions I initially wanted the Lord to answer came in His timing. He did not answer them all right away, because He wanted the time with me. When the time was right, He revealed my passions, identity and freed me to start the new beginnings He desired. It was a powerful vision for me. I did not want to get stuck in the mentality that my life did not have anything to offer. My life offered the resurrection power of His life. Living a life through Him assured many hopeful promises.

Before I ever entered into my healing journey, I was stuck in this box mentality. I limited my own future. It took this revelation for me to see the endless possibilities God had for me. I always had compassion for animals. I loved learning about them. In fact, God used animals throughout my healing journey. They were very intuitive to my feelings. Since a child, I had a deep love for animals. However, I never thought God would open doors for me to work with them. Just as I placed myself in a box, I also put God in a box. There are countless ministry opportunities, as long as God is in our heart. I use to think ministry was work that rarely involved passions. I found myself forcing a round peg in a square hole, just to fit into ministry. In fact, I applied to be in a ministry position. God removed me from that spot, and I was very grateful. I was planning my life around what other people thought I should do for ministry. I was taught that the "calling" of my life was a job. It was only through this process that I realized the "call" of my life is to follow Jesus. If I would have stayed in my "calling", as others saw it, I would have missed out on a fulfilling life trusting in Jesus. Ministry is everywhere. Ministry should come out of our relationship and love with Christ. I used to hear, walk in the "fruit" of God. Where is the "fruit" of your work? I realized the fruit comes from the branch. The branch is connected to the vine. I don't produce the "fruit", God does. It is not in my power, it is being in the presence of God that produces fruit. We get deceived when people say, produce "fruit". *I am the vine; you are the branches. If a man remains in me and I in him, he will bear much fruit; apart from me you can do nothing. (John 15:5)*

I was learning an extensive amount of information from this vision with the bird. As I was soaking in the wisdom from Jesus, I noticed the bird again feeding out of His hand. I looked down to the hand of God and I witnessed continued provision for the bird. It seemed as if the bird seed was endless. I was grasping the endless provision Jesus has for me. The bird flew and repositioned himself in the tree. At that point, I realized we were encircled by creatures of all kinds. Some animals I recognized. There were animals close to my heart, even animals I called my own. I knew them by name. There were other animals I had never laid eyes on before in my entire earthly existence. I was fascinated with their appearance. I wasn't frightened by their presence. I understood that the things of earth are limited, and there are far greater and exciting things we can anticipate in Heaven. The Lord spoke as he positioned Himself in the center. He reminded me that I was in the midst of my passions. It seemed as if this vision was now full circle. I gained a tremendous amount of insight.

In the distance I viewed the old shack. This time, I was able to have a new understanding. The shack represented my heart, identity and dreams. As we both glanced at the near collapse of the shack, He gently touched my spirit. The enemy came to destroy my life, dreams and relationship with Him. But, the Lord comes to bring me abundant life. He is rebuilding my foundation. He is building me up with His righteous right hand. *I took you from the ends of the earth; from its farthest corners I called you. I said, "You are my servant" I have chosen you and have not rejected you. So do not fear, for I am with you; do not be dismayed, for I am your God. I will strengthen you and help you; I will uphold you with my righteous right hand. (Isaiah 41:9)*

CHAPTER 15

HIGHWAY TO HOLINESS

I was sitting alone in my room seeking the Lord. I had my time of worship and prayer. But now, I sat waiting on the Lord. My eyes were closed, and this all consuming light began to blind me. I was lying on the floor and began to feel a peace resonate within my spirit. I quieted my mind and softly invited the Holy Spirit to come and speak and minister to me. I saw myself as if I became a third person. I felt like I was walking into the center of the sun. In an instant, I retracted myself from this vision. My eyes were still closed, and I was still seeking the Lord. I wondered what this vision meant. Where am I? A gentle voice in my heart resonated when I felt the tenderness of the Lord speaking over me. Jesus said, "You are in my glory". With the knowledge of being in the glory of God, my body began to tremble. An overwhelming sense of emotions seemed to invade me. I was fearful and excited at the same time. The light made it difficult to outline His face, but I saw a silhouette of a man. With a tender and loving voice, He spoke my name and powerfully declared, "Darkness does not have a hold on me." His truth pierced me. Almost as if a large, spiritual sword severed me from my past. I wept. Instantaneously, I felt released from all harm, threats, darkness and chains. I felt freedom, joy and victory. I was in awe. Nothing could overpower me now. I could hardly stand in His presence. Tears that streamlined down my face were not tears of pain, but tears of joy from the freedom that penetrated a once broken soul. His words were like a sword that severed me from darkness and placed me in His glory. I was so weak in His presence, yet I was becoming strong in His truth. I had momentarily looked down; perhaps it was to reassure myself that this was real. When I turned my eyes up to Him I recognized His slow movement in another direction. His presence moved ahead. I had an immediate desire to follow Him. As I walked behind Him, I noticed an astonishing pathway before me. His presence made a clear and concise trail to follow. Although by now He was much further ahead, I knew there was a reason to follow Him.

I saw in my steps ahead a long gravel road. Off in the distance, it veered slightly to the left. I could not see the end. My mind began to battle with the flesh, speaking to me, "You have errands to run, you have other things to do." Despite my mind and the doubts it created in me, I allowed my spirit to continue its journey within.

I stood on the road. Staring ahead, I began to walk. I didn't see Christ there, and I didn't know where this road was leading. But in my spirit I knew I needed to see whatever the Lord wanted to show me. I took my first step, and my eyes opened to new sights. On each side of the road stood countless angels lined shoulder to shoulder as far as I could see. I took a breath in, amazed at these strong statured, angelic beings. Some towered with massive wings covering over their bodies. Some were wearing magnificent head pieces that displayed power and fortitude. Others had simple, pure garland wreaths of olive leaves wrapped around their crowns. I was in awe of their appearance. I always imagined angels to be strong warriors with oversized muscles and wings. Some angels were exactly that. Many angels appeared to have obvious war wounds from battles. I recognized the scars that covered some of the angels were marks of protection over my life. Although many were of great strength, there were also angels that were smaller in size. I identified their mission to be different in my life than some of the other angels. I couldn't see the definition and detail of their faces, but I was able to detect the service they provided me. Their service was unto the Lord and each angel had a purposeful mission in my life. Their beauty seemed Holy and pure. I imagine it is because of their worshipful service to Christ. I slowly placed one foot in front of the other, realizing there was not a moment of time in my life that I did not have angels by my side. I was amazed by what my spirit was seeing. Surprisingly, the angels seemed to applaud and honor me, as I passed along the road. The power of His army of angels protected my life when I seemed vulnerable. I was able to glimpse into a spiritual walk of my life. The angels surrounded me in the past, present and future path. There was not one moment or gap between the angels. As far as I could see, there were angels along this path. They clearly knew who I was, and the mission that they had was accomplished for the greater purpose of our creator. So much was communicated and experienced in a short amount of time. I began to see that His timing is far different then my timing. His timing demonstrated power and effectiveness. I learned more can be accomplished in a short amount of time in powerful prayer, and time in His presence, than a whole days worth of work in counseling. I don't want to minimize counseling, but I want to maximize the accomplishments made in His presence.

I continued down this long gravel road. I was able to see the end. What stood before me is nearly impossible to describe. This place appeared to be a throne room. It had the presence of royalty. I stood before a chair and a large foot. I could only see the base of this prestigious, royal chair. Even though I was at a distance from the chair, the size and magnitude of this chair and foot was beyond my comprehension. I turned my head side to side, and up and down. In my own scope of vision, I could not grasp the immeasurable size of this foot.

I stood quietly. Then the great and mighty foot stepped down in my direction. The colossal figure stepped down from this "throne" and became human-sized. The Lord God stepped down off His throne to change my life. He became my size, in order for me to relate to Him. He stood before me, right in front of me. He welcomed me. My knees became weak and I trembled in His presence. I recognized Him from many of my visions during my healing process. I always knew it was Jesus who rescued me, but it was an entirely different circumstance standing before Him now. Emotions overwhelmed me. All my worries, doubts and pain seemed to be forgotten. Every act of injustice forced upon me, was rectified. His presence washed and renewed me. He cleansed me of the sickness, and the grime of unwanted abuse. It was such a powerful moment in my life. I experienced a love that will never be forgotten. I felt alive. Peace overcame me and joy filled my soul. I stood before my Savior and looked into His eyes. For a brief moment I saw into the eyes of Jesus. His eyes were a sea of compassion overflowing in every movement of His fixation towards me. The depth of His eyes foretold His deep passion of love that sought after me, my entire life. I saw fire in His eyes. I saw pleasure in His eyes. I saw depth of grace beyond my understanding. His eyes were inviting. In His eyes I saw an immense desire to protect. His look of love captivated me. I longed to see more of His beauty. Although I received so much from looking into His eyes, it was actually just a brief moment in time. But that brief moment is unforgettable.

I was caught up in the love and justice of Jesus. My emotions overcame me and I stood worshipping Him. Before I knew it, He was on His knees. I thought for a moment that my mind had overstepped the boundaries. Maybe, I was imagining this now. It was so powerful a minute ago, but now I have gone too far? Why would God be on His knees before me? Was pride entering in? I continued to worship Him in humility, and the same vision of Jesus on His knees came back. Why would Jesus be on His knees? This isn't real. I ignored all the lies entering in my mind and made the decision to trust the Lord's leading.

He rose to His feet and there appeared a crown in His hands. I stood quietly, anticipating His next move. I never saw the crown before. I didn't know He had it, but that was irrelevant. What was He doing with a crown? He lifted His arms, and then His hands above my head. He was still holding the crown. He slowly rested it upon my head. My heart melted with unbelief. I don't deserve this. I must be making this up. I silenced my thoughts and breathed in as if I was taking every second of this time to cherish in my heart. I felt the sorrows of my life slip away and His great pleasure seemed to rest on my head. This powerful encounter led me to an intimate place of His glory. My body, mind, and spirit were completely captivated by His love. This encounter affected me to the core. I felt freedom harvested within me. I was weak, yet I felt strong.

In all my healing, I had very few encounters as powerful as this one. Each one brought healing and truth. Each one also required me to align the experience with the Word of God. So I began to pray to the Lord. I said, "Lord, if this encounter was true, show me in your Word." In the quietness of my heart and my room, I received confirmation. I felt this gentle leading to turn my Bible to Isaiah 35. I began to read the passage.

They will see the glory of the Lord, the splendor of our God. Strengthen the knees that give way; say to those with fearful hearts, Be strong, do not fear' your God will come, he will come with vengeance, with divine retribution he will come to save you. Then will the eyes of the blind be opened and the ears of the deaf unstopped. Then will the lame leap like a deer, and the mute tongue shout for joy. Water will gush forth in the wilderness and streams in the desert. The burning sand will become a pool, the thirsty ground bubbling springs. Vs. 8 and a highway will be there. It will be called the Way of Holiness. The unclean will not journey on it, it will be for those who walk in that Way; wicked fools will not go about on it. No lion will be there, nor will any ferocious beast get up on it; they will not be found there. But only the redeemed will walk there, and the ransomed of the Lord will return. They will enter Zion with singing; everlasting joy will crown their heads. Gladness and joy will overtake them and sorrow and sighing will flee away. (Isaiah 35: 2-10)

In that moment, the Lord showed me that I no longer needed to be afraid. He has sent His angels to watch over me. I will walk on the way of holiness, and no wicked person from my past will overpower me. I am redeemed by the blood of the Lamb. I have been ransomed from my grave. I am His. I will enter into Zion with singing, and everlasting joy will crown my head. The Lord removed my sorrows and pain. The affliction of my past is gone. All the darkness has been exchanged for an eternal life and joy. Darkness no longer has a hold on me.

CHAPTER 16

CONCLUSION

Regardless of our circumstances, faith will be a fundamental requirement to get us through. The world says we must, "See to believe". God's ways are that we must believe in order to see. I know there were countless times when friends dismissed the process of healing. I had good friends reject, accuse, and abandon me, because they did not see. It was an arduous season, when the storms seemed to twist and turn every day. I knew the Lord directed me in this path. Although many times I wanted to give up, I tried daily to believe there was a hope for tomorrow. I had to believe there was freedom in Christ, before I could actually see the freedom He had for me. I know the struggle to walk in faith. I know the strong desire to want to see results. However, God calls each of us to believe, when we cannot see. Then, when we follow His footsteps regardless of our sight and desires, He reveals the promises of hope and a new day. He is faithful to deliver us. He is faithful to reward our faith, giving us the opportunity to finally see, what we held on to believe.

I know there are countless professional and beneficial methods of healing. I have tried many of them. Although there were successful moments, none truly compared to the power of prayer and patience in the Lord. I know that in my suffering, my faith has been refined. God has made me prosperous through my suffering. *It is because God has made me fruitful in the land of my suffering. (Genesis 41:52)* When I submitted my afflictions to Christ, I found eternal life. *Therefore I am now going to allure her; I will lead her into the desert and speak tenderly to her. There I will give her back her vineyards, and will make the Valley of Achor a door of hope. (Hosea 2:14)* When we find ourselves isolated and alone, we have the opportunity to quiet our spirit, and sit in His presence. It is in our desert experience He provides streams of life. *Water will gush forth in the wilderness and streams in the desert.(Isaiah 35:6)*

Our doors of hope, and streams of life, come through the refining impact of God. I believe that maturity should not be measured solely by the number of years one has followed the Lord, or by the number of years assigned by our age. Maturity should be measured by the experiences in our lives that we allow the power of God to impact us. Too often we are not impacted by God. We do not allow time in our lives for God to really make changes in our hearts. Impact is a collision course in which a direction is changed. Changing direction requires faith. Faith pleases God.

If we desire for God to work in our lives, we need to remember, He will only be able to work in the areas we surrender to Him. He will not force Himself upon us. The path of freedom requires; silence before the Lord, trust in Him, and dedication to work hard. Freedom comes from His work within our hearts. Freedom from our circumstances might lead to temporary satisfaction, but will still need deeper work.

In order to receive healing, we must recognize and take responsibility for our bondage. We live out what we believe. Therefore if you believe lies, you are living lies. If you believe the truth of Jesus and who you are in Christ, then you are living out a life through Jesus. Jesus is truth. *I am the way and the truth and the life. No one comes to the Father except through me. (John 14:6)*

I will never tell all the torment I have suffered at the hands of evil. It was not my intention to describe the evil that oppressed me. The suffering mentioned in this book is only to provide a baseline, in order to understand the many times God liberated me. It was not my desire to give credit to the ritual acts, of the occult. The purpose of this book is to say I am alive, because God's hand was upon me. It is a miracle. It was never through my own power to overcome. My victory has been empowered through Jesus. Through God we can escape addictions, trauma, abuse, depression, sexual immorality, and severe torture. He is the "ONE WAY OUT". My heart's desire is to display the mighty work of Christ. We can receive freedom and deliverance through the blood of Jesus. The enemy clearly wanted to destroy me. God clearly desired for me to live. *They overcame him by the blood of the Lamb and by the word of their testimony. (Revelation 12:11)*

Every detail of this book came from real experiences. Each vision imparted was truly a life changing encounter with Christ. I would have never imagined such a glorious life. Every vision was spectacular, but experiencing the presence of the Lord is unmatched by any words.

In all the scriptures outlined in this book, one of my favorites is: *My ears have heard of you but now my eyes have seen you. (Job 42:5)* In all the horrendous abuse, spiritual oppression and near death experiences, I would not exchange my life, for the knowledge I have of Christ Jesus. From Job, a Biblical man who understood affliction, sorrow and pain, to my life experience, I will say Jesus is worth it all. I would never have imagined what my eyes have seen, or what my spirit has encountered. Jesus is the only way. And now, just as Job experienced the latter day blessings, so will all those who have suffered, and committed their journey to Christ. *They will be called the Holy People, the Redeemed of the Lord; and you will be called Sought After, the City No Longer Deserted. Isaiah (62:12)*

END NOTES

WALKING IN AUTHORITY, VISIONS AND PROPHECY

Although I am not an expert on authority in Christ, I have had countless interactions that required me to exercise authority in Christ, in order to experience freedom. Walking in authority never comes from our own power. *Not by might or by power, but by my Spirit says the Lord. (Zech 4:6)* Operating in the authority of Christ comes from humble submission to Him. His power is unlimited. When we humble ourselves to the Lord and His power, we are able to trample over evil. *I saw Satan fall like lightening from heaven. I have given you authority to trample on snakes and scorpions and to overcome all the power of the enemy; nothing will harm you. (Luke 10:18, 19)*

First of all, God has all authority over Heaven and earth. *Therefore God exalted Him to the highest place and gave Him the name that is above every name, that at the name of Jesus every knee should bow, in heaven and on earth and under the earth, and every tongue confess that Jesus Christ is Lord. (Phil 2:9-11) Jesus Christ who has gone into heaven and is at God's right hand—with angels, authorities and powers in submission to Him. (1 Peter 3:22)* In order to walk in the authority of Christ, you must be true followers of Jesus Christ. His written word is true. *As for God, his way is perfect; the word of the Lord is flawless. (2Sam 22:3)*

Second, claiming the scripture is a powerful, effective and necessary tool. *For the word of God is living and active. Sharper than any double-*

edged sword, it penetrates even to dividing soul and spirit, joints and marrow; it judges the thoughts and attitudes of the heart. (Hebrews 4:12)

Third of all, it is important to know that you are not waging war against the person. If a person is wrestling with spiritual oppression, you don't need to yell at any demonic spirit. You don't have to throw a person to the ground. You simply exercise your authority in Christ Jesus and command the demonic spirit to leave

Finally, be strong in the Lord and in his mighty power. Put on the full armor of God so that you can take your stand against the devil's schemes. For our struggle is not against flesh and blood, but against the rulers, against the authorities, against the powers of this dark world and against the spiritual forces of evil in the heavenly realms. Therefore put on the full armor of God, so that when the day of evil comes, you may be able to stand your ground, and after you have done everything, to stand. Stand firm then, with the belt of truth buckled around your waist, with the breastplate of righteousness in place, and with your feet fitted with the readiness that comes from the gospel of peace. In addition to all this, take up the shield of faith, with which you can extinguish all the flaming arrows of the evil one. Take the helmet of salvation and the sword of the Spirit, which is the word of God. And pray in the Spirit on all occasions with all kinds of prayers and requests. With this in mind, be alert and always keep on praying for all the saints. (Ephesians 6:10-18)

Finally, I realized some vital principles in my journey. Just as there is a hierarchy of angels, so there is with evil. *But even the archangel Michael, when he was disputing with the devil about the body of Moses, did not dare to bring a slanderous accusation against him, but said, "The Lord rebuke you!" (Jude 9)* You can rebuke, silence, cast out; bind the enemy in Jesus name. In going through deliverance, it is imperative to ask the Lord if there are any grounds in which the enemy has a foothold. Seek the Lord to fight and judge on your behalf. Invite the power of the Holy Spirit to intervene. Repentance is crucial. Forgiveness is essential. Following the Lord is necessary. You do not need to be afraid. When you exercise your authority in the name and by the blood of Jesus, any harassing spirit of darkness must flee. It does not require shouting or a "Hollywood" show. A person will experience freedom and peace in deliverance. Use scripture, sing worship songs, pray in the Spirit. I found these tools very beneficial.

Prophetic Tools

I believe prophecy can minister to a body of believers and to individuals, serving purposes of encouragement, revelation and comfort to the body of Christ. I personally believe the spirit and gift of prophecy still occurs in our day. It is a gift that supernaturally imparts God's word of truth to His believers. It comes through the discernment and knowledge of His voice, and empowers the individual with the gifting, to speak what the Lord desires His people to know.

There are various levels of prophecy. These levels of prophecy and different styles of prophecy are recorded in the Bible. Listed below are only some of the various levels of prophecy.

- Spirit of prophecy: a prophetic spirit that is present amongst a group (1 Sam 19:20)
- Gift of prophecy: manifests in an individual through various forms delivering a spoken word from God. (1 Corinthians 12:10)
- Prophetic Mantle: A mantle of authority resting on an individual (Elijah to Elisha)
- Office of prophecy: An accountable and consistent prophet (Ephesians 4:11)

Along with the various levels of prophecy, below are some different types and styles of prophecy.

- Seer: (vision) the ability to see in the spiritual realm or use prophetic gifting through the avenue of pictures, dreams and mental images (1 Samuel 9:9, Revelation 4:1)
- Governmental prophecy: (Daniel spoke of government changes and order)
- Counsel: The ability to correct someone and release a measure of grace over them
- Weeping/ Travailing: Jeremiah
- Administrative and Finance: Joseph's ability to speak in authority of economic hardship

People who operate in the prophetic gift should:

- Live a life with accountability and devotion through seeking His truth
- First be an intercessor in order to be a prophet. You cannot prophesy without a dedicated life of intercession
- Prophetic people are sometimes treated differently and need to develop a tough skin Avoid emotions getting in the way, when being misunderstood
- People who desire to speak God's word should never include a personal interpretation. In other words, don't include your thoughts at the end of what God is communicating. Don't mix His words and your interpretation
- Prophetic people are sensitive to the Holy Spirit and will often have a form of manifestation of confirmation with what the Spirit is speaking. For instance, whenever I was around someone who seemed to give me a check in my spirit, I would often get sick to my stomach, sore throat, dizzy or smell something offensive

Here are some solid foundations if you are seeking the prophetic gift.

- Be very precise with words and humble in your heart
- Allow God to always work in your life
- Ask God to expose any sin in your life
- Walk in forgiveness and repentance
- Everything that is prophesied must agree with the written word of God
- Always ask God for timing to release His word
- When our quiet time with the Lord decreases, often our hearing will become dull
- Make praying, repentance, humility, forgiveness and worship a lifestyle
- Seek the Lord, not the gift. The gift comes from first seeking God

The Bible mentions and supports the gift of prophecy through several Old and New Testament scriptures. (Revelation 4:1, Daniel, Job 42:5, Acts 2:17, Ezekiel 1:1)

The most important aspect with operating in the prophetic gift is; relationship with the Lord.

Lord, Lord did we not prophesy in your name, and in your
In your name drive out demons and perform many miracles?
Then I will tell them plainly, I never knew you. Away from
Me, you evildoers! (Matthew 7:22-23)

SRA, PTSD

The word "occult" means secret and hidden. Therefore, the word itself gives explanation that ritual abuse is not acknowledged in the open. Satanic ritual abuse (SRA) is highly secretive, and often entangled with dangerous threats. Those who understand the operation of the occult's agenda recognize the power behind the threats, trapping many to keep silent of the horrifying abuse, and hide any possible evidence. I cannot prove all stories as truth or not. However, there is an underlining element of both factual and experiential knowledge that just cannot be denied.

The Occult is a large society filled with people of various positions. These people hold a status in governmental and military positions, business leaders, pastors, missionaries, and teachers, to name a few. Occult members are not restricted by any limitations. However, the higher their position of influence, the greater likelihood of involvement can increase. Not everybody is involved, but an agenda of the occult is to use people in power. I am not declaring that all pastors or leaders are involved in the occult. However, I don't dismiss the idea that Christians are not involved. (Use discernment and ask the Lord for wisdom). There are a high number of male and female perpetrators professing Christian values. In fact, a significant amount of my abuse came from church leaders, board members, Christian parents, and ministry staff.

On a small scale, satanic rituals can consist of, but are not limited to people participating in; dungeon and dragons, witchcraft, séance, and black and white magic. On a larger scale, abuse includes some of the following horrible and unthinkable human and animal suffering.

The following material is sensitive and graphic. **Please do not read if you are currently seeking healing and recovery with SRA.** Many SRA victims have claimed to have similar or exact traumatizing events occur through a forced participation in ritual activity.

- Drinking of blood, semen, urine or other body fluids
- Spinning upside down or left hanging upside down
- Experiences of near drowning or being partially buried alive
- Skinning or burning, branding, blinding lights
- Forced to perform sexual acts with same and/or opposite sexual partner, family members or bestiality
- Using objects such as spiders snakes or mice to trap or place on the victim's body creating extreme phobias
- Being trapped underground, in sheds, closets, coffins or other small confined areas
- Witnessing and participating in animal and human sacrifices
- Summoning demonic and satanic presence and dark spiritual powers
- Symbolic and modified crucifixion
- Bondage using ropes, wire, cable, handcuffs and other methods to tie a victim
- Electrocution using an active current around body, limbs and head to conduct electricity
- Using inhumane techniques such as cattle prods, whips and barbed wire to threaten a victim
- Sleep and sensory deprivation
- Use of mental programming through threats, images and torment to traumatize and fragment the brain
- Forcing people to make vows, oaths and covenants with Satan
- Forcing people to worship Satan
- Confusing people's beliefs about the One True God
- Twisting or misusing Biblical scripture
- Impregnating and aborting fetus' in women

Often SRA survivors will experience some of the following list. This list only includes some of the associated symptoms of an SRA individual.

- Victims are often excellent survivors, with an above average intelligence
- A strong sense of justice and victim and animal advocacy
- They will often enter careers to help wounded people
- May show severe signs of anxiety and depression and battle constantly with suicidal tendencies
- An individual will struggle with retrieving childhood memories, some specific to time or ages
- An individual will often have dissociated identity disorder
- Extreme mistrust of people, God and people in authoritative positions
- They will experience extreme phobias ranging from insects and snakes to balloons, food, confinement, birthdays, doctors and more
- Often a survivor will complain of random body pains, migraines, digestive problems, constipation and multiple eating and sleep disorders
- A survivor may have inappropriate sexual behavior or habits that seem uncontrollable.
- A survivor may also struggle with making decisions or the ability to defend oneself or stand up for oneself
- A survivor may also have hyper vigilance and have sensitive startle responses.
- A survivor may experience loss of time
- A survivor will also have a history of self mutilation and demonstrate an interest in knives, scissors and blades and other weapons
- A survivor will have a high pain tolerance and often not be aware of any injury

SRA will tremendously damage a person's (spiritual, cognitive and emotional) growth, development, identity, decision making process and normal social interaction. It will affect an individual's perception of God, trust, safety, value, and attachment in both companionship and intimate relationships. It will often lead to an extended amount of intervention both medically and psychologically. If not recognized early, it can provoke behavioral tendencies such as, suicidal thoughts, extreme anxiety, depression, violence, rage, hatred, addictive patterns, sexual misconduct and much more. 1

DID

Dissociation is a separation of elements from the traumatizing event. Dissociation reduces the impact of the experience. This coping mechanism allows the person to remain partially functional. Dissociation can cause people to have alterations in their brains. 2 Dissociative Identity Disorder leaves a victim with fragmented sense of self and identity. 3

PTSD

Post traumatic stress disorder (PTSD) is often found in those who have incurred a significant amount of trauma through war, natural disasters, accidents, rape, abuse and violence. It is more common in our present day world and has significantly increased in our culture today.

Trauma disrupts the entire nervous system and often hinders a person from processing and integrating memories into a conscious mentality. Trauma will create chaos in our brains, possibly leaving a person with a fragmented identity, (DID) anxiety, depression, suicidal tendencies, loss of memory and much more. A person that suffers from PTSD can incur the following symptoms: nightmares, flashbacks, difficulty with memory and concentrating, hyper arousal, hyper vigilant, avoidance, triggers, isolation and extreme phobias.

Through medical and psychological research, trauma has been linked to long term wounding, that greatly effects regular adaptations to people's everyday lives. Trauma can have a damaging effect on our brain. First, our brain is separated by a right and left hemisphere. The right side of our brain holds the senses, images, creativity and themes in our lives. The left side holds the logic, linguistics, and critical thinking. When trauma occurs it splits or disconnects the communication of the right and left hemisphere of the brain. Trauma paralyzes the thinking process, and relies on the brain's right side to ignite the survival mode.

During specific studies of patients suffering from severe trauma, researchers were able to detect activity of left side of the brain diminished (the logical side), while the right hemisphere, specifically the amygdala lit up. The amygdala is a small almond shape portion in the brain that gives meaning to an event. The amygdala is the "alarm" in our brain that deciphers if the information that is being received is safe or dangerous. It is also contains the emotional experience during a traumatic event and memory recall. It will often become sensitive or active during a trauma. By remembering a traumatic incident this portion of the brain creates behavioral "red flags" or what others refer to as "triggers". A "trigger" is when the amygdala over- responds to a present day situation caused by a previous traumatic event. The amygdala does not function or cooperate with cognitive functions. It is a portion of the brain that controls emotional reactions. When going through a healing process of trauma, the words of the trauma often are shut down. However, the picture of the memory surfaces likes snapshots in a silent film.

The hypothalamus is the portion of our brain that receives sensory input. It receives information from our sight, smell, touch, taste, and hearing. It then delivers the information to the brain to be processed.

The Hippocampus involves memory and encodes information such as: feelings, thoughts, past facts and experiences. The Hippocampus has been referred to as the "librarian" of our brain. It has been linked to memory more than any other structure of the brain. It acts as a control center, instead of a storage unit. However, the Hippocampus is also a portion of the brain used during memory recall. It knows where the memory has been stored and is able to pull the event up like a librarian pulling a book from a shelf.

The Frontal Cortex is known to be a portion of the brain that supervises the entire process of integration between cognition and emotions. It has been mentioned that the Frontal Cortex is able to distinguish between a real or false threat.

The Corpus Callosum is an area of the brain that connects the right and left hemisphere, allowing communication between the two hemispheres.

Our brain is a very complex organ with many different operating systems still being studied. Memory and cognition involve various components of the brain in order for input to be processed and memory to be recalled. Our brain is also an amazing organ which enables individuals to cope and survive during trauma. Although, I only understand a small fraction of the complexity of our minds during trauma, I will make a basic outline of the functioning of our brain when trauma occurs. First, the input and traumatic event is processed by the hypothalamus. It receives the information through our sensory input. It then proceeds to the amygdala determining if there is danger in the situation. At that point, the traumatic event is processed by simultaneous events of the brain. A nerve coming from the brain to the adrenal glands rapidly begin to secrete adrenaline (cortisol) through the blood stream, causing the heart to beat faster and the alert the body of an emergency. The flood of hormones create a response known to many as "fight or flight". While this process is occurring, the left side of the brain decreases its functioning while the right side of the brain seems to respond. This results in an increased emotional response and visual sense, while the linguistics and critical thinking decrease.

Memory

Although this is a simplified version of a very complex system at work, I will try to point out some key factors when working through trauma. First of all, memory is a function of the brain that empowers us to store and retrieve information. There are several types of memories along with different mechanisms to the retrieval process. Overall, several doctors and scientists have agreed upon the existence of somatic memory (cellular or muscle memory), sensory memory (taste, visual, tactile), and conceptual memory (episodic, procedural, declarative). In particular, in relation to trauma, it is important to recognize that trauma is an event(s) which affects the entire body, especially the nervous system. Therefore, recalling traumatic events will perhaps include various forms of memory. In order to assure an accurate memory, let me share briefly some elements that will hopefully enlighten the integrity and actuality of a memory.

Trauma will sometimes dissociate a person's mind, (DID) leaving a fragmented mind, memory and individual. The victim of trauma can experience: numbness, splintered identity, lack of verbal recall and more. When the trauma occurs, the most responsive portion of our brain is not language and thinking. Instead, it is the pictures, emotions and sensory information. Therefore, a memory will be a visual and emotional snapshot of an incident, rather than a detailed and descriptive statement. The memory might initiate a smell, taste or body pain, (muscle and sensory), rather than a specific detail, that use the thinking and logical portion of our brain. In memory recall of a traumatic event, there is a rush of hormones that creates a "fight or flight" feeling. It will often ignite memory in a single picture, co-insiding with emotions such as: fear, abandonment, and anger.

Somatic memory is defined as retaining the trauma, or impact of injury within the muscles. It has been researched, and found helpful to treat and release the somatic memories in order for the individual to receive complete healing from the trauma. Somatic memories embody traumatic events, (emotional) as well as physical injuries such as: physical trauma, rape, sport or car accidents. Somatic memory suggests that cells of the human body retain the memories of the event in the muscles as well as the brain. Somatic memories indicate that during the episode of trauma, when the body goes into "fight or flight", a flood of chemicals are released. This flood resonates throughout the entire body, and the release of these chemicals (along with muscle tension) can become trapped in an area of injury. Somatic memories if accepted as a source of confirmation or predication of an event can be difficult to override. Once it has been stored, it can be a reliable source or indication of a traumatic event.

Counseling Suggestions

For those who desire to counsel someone through trauma, let me suggest some counseling tips. Whether it is a friend, co-worker or a lay counselor through your church or ministry organization there are some vital steps to consider. First of all, the most important step is to yield to Christ's leading. If you are working through a traumatic event with an individual be sure to include the following in a therapy session:
- Yield to God's voice and leading
- Listen intently
- Compassionately synchronize or empathize
- Validate them and the pain they have experienced
- Begin restoring the person with truth

- Be patient. It is about God's timing, His will, His healing. Often, we want another person to be healed immediately but God has valuables within the journey.

I don't believe you have to be a licensed counselor to help people through trauma. I believe having a degree can be both a negative and positive tool for an individual seeking healing and truth. However, if you are a lay person in your church or ministry organization and have been presented with an opportunity to help someone through satanic ritual abuse, please consider the following suggestions as strong and valid requirements prior to starting any healing journey.

- You must be clearly led by the Lord
- You must be a strong and mature Christian to help anyone through ritual abuse
- You must be willing to go to truth and work through any unresolved wounds in your own personal life
- You must develop a support team who will be committed to intercede for your counseling sessions, listen as you debrief, be trustworthy, ensuring safety and confidentiality for you and the counselee
- If you are able, seek professional advice from a counselor in order to have better insight on the validity of stories, and operations of occult activity
- Trust in the Lord
- Follow the Holy Spirit
- Understand it will be a lengthy and intense process

Here is a list of instrumental tools practiced in my healing sessions:

- Warfare, taking authority over spiritual darkness, deliverance
- Repentance, Forgiveness, giving pain to Christ
- Reading and declaring His written Word
- Waiting and listening, following the Holy Spirit
- Confirming visions with the Word of God
- Nurturing, parental guidance, balance fun with various friends and activities

- Empathy, validation, synchronization, patience, consistency, wisdom, time
- Exercise, rewards, diligence, faith, accountability
- Trusting in God
- Intercession

In prayer there are a few important keys to effective healing;

- Submit to the Lord
- Humility
- Pray the blood and covering of Jesus over you, the counselee and all your time, property, assets and loved ones
- Pray to break off from spiritual darkness, lies, harassment, and all ritual activities, and false gods
- Pray giving permission for Christ to work, lead and bring truth in the survivor's life
- Pray in authority, pray for wisdom and discernment
- Follow the leading of the Holy Spirit
- Pray for confirmation in His word, that God would bring clarity

REFERENCES

1) Jim W. Goll, (2004). The Seer: The Prophetic Power of Visions, Dreams, and Open Heavens. Shippensburg, PA: Destiny Image Publishers, Inc. Pages 116-127

2) Ellen P. Lacter, Ph.D., (March 4, 2004). Kinds of Torture Endured in Ritual Abuse and Trauma Based Mind Control. Retrieved from website: http://endritualabuse.org

3) Theresa Burke, Ph.D., (copyright 2010). How Trauma Impacts the Brain. Retrieved from website: http://www.rachelsvineyard.org

4) J. Douglas Bremner, M. D., The Lasting Effects on Psychological Trauma on Memory and the Hippocampus. "Stressing the Point". Retrieved from website: http://lawandpsychiatry.com

5) Alexander, (July 9, 2010). How Memories Are Made. Retrieved from website: http:// www.memoryzine.com

6) Pamela Perez, (October 4, 2004). Somatic Memory. Body Memories. Retrieved from website: http://www.suite101.com/article.cfm/did/111512/1

7) Faith Allen, (March 27, 2008). What is a Body Memory? Retrieved from website: http://faithallen.wordpress.com

CPSIA information can be obtained at www.ICGtesting.com
Printed in the USA
BVOW041139130911

271061BV00001B/6/P